Parking Lot Rules

&

75 Other Ideas for Raising
Amazing Children

To Mandongh —

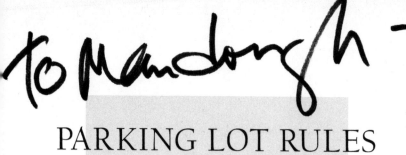

PARKING LOT RULES

&

75 Other Ideas for Raising Amazing Children

TOM STURGES

BALLANTINE BOOKS · NEW YORK

Copyright © 2008 by Tom Sturges

Published in the United States by Ballantine Books, an imprint of
The Random House Publishing Group, a division of
Random House, Inc., New York.

BALLANTINE and colophon are registered trademarks of
Random House, Inc.

Photograph on title page by Antonina Armato

LIBRARY OF CONGRESS CATALOGING-IN-PUBLICATION DATA
Sturges, Tom.
Parking lot rules & 75 other ideas for raising amazing children
/Tom Sturges.
p. cm.
ISBN 978-0-345-50373-2
1. Child rearing.   I. Title.
HQ769.S934 2008
649'.1—dc22   2008002390

Printed in the United States of America on acid-free paper

www.ballantinebooks.com

2 4 6 8 9 7 5 3 1

FIRST EDITION

Book design by Simon M. Sullivan

THIS BOOK IS DEDICATED . . .

To my two amazing sons, Thomas and Sam. There has been no greater joy or honor in this life than being your father. You will only understand the depth of this emotion when you get to know your own children, but take my word for it, it is unbelievable how much you can love somebody.

To my first great love and closest ally for almost all of my existence, my dearest mother, Sandy Sturges. Not a day goes by when I do not think of you still.

To Antonina Armato. One of the richest relationships I will ever know is the one I share with you . . . as writer, fiancée, wife, mother of my two sons, partner in their raising, caretaker of my mama on her deathbed, and now ex-wife and friend for life.

Foreword
ELI LIEBER, PH.D.

I was flattered to be invited to read Tom Sturges's manuscript. Tom and I have known each other for a number of years as parents raising our children in the same community. Our boys attend school together. Both of our families are regularly present and busy in the community. You can't help but get to know the families who *are*, because—like them or not—you keep seeing them contribute their time, energy, skills, and other assets to schools, sports programs, and events in your community.

Focused on the well-being of children, I've spent many years as a professional social science researcher of parenting styles and practices and how they affect the environments in which children develop. Involved in this work from psychological, anthropological, and cultural perspectives, I have learned that there are many ways to be a successful parent. Communication is where I start, and that's one reason why chapter 2 in *Parking Lot Rules* resonates with me to my core. Here Tom tosses out clever ideas about engaging and being engaged with your child, and shows that you can have a great time getting to know your children and helping them get to know themselves.

Through the realities of my work I have learned that there are many different degrees and forms of parenting challenges, and many ways to struggle with them. I typically focus on families dealing with a particular type of challenge, and I search, amid their struggles, for signs of success so we can learn as much as possible about what's going *right*. Illustrative cases of success can be shared with those facing similar challenges, to help them try to solve their problems. It's true that what works for some cannot be expected to work for everyone, but watching and learning from successful models is a great way to witness creative problem solving in real-life action.

We all want to guide our children, but as we know, this requires self-control. Tougher still is the fact that when we get busy, hungry, tired, or distracted, our patience and thoughtfulness can go out the window—as does our poise when disciplining our children. The one passage I drew big circles around in *Parking Lot Rules* was this chapter 5 quote: "The power of forgiveness can make everything right again." Brain surgery? I don't think so, but this just got me, and it's a great example of how Tom reminds us of the fundamentals. No matter the extent of our dedication, love, or experience, there are times when we can all use a little reminder of what we expect of our children and ourselves.

I write here not just as an academic, but also as a father of four lovely children, as a husband, a friend, and a person who cares about the well-being of the children around me. You could say I am an interested observer of people such as Tom and of their activities in the community that affect children. Like those positive models I look for in my work, *Parking Lot Rules* provides a great example of success.

With heartfelt warmth and an entertaining, engaging style, Tom shares his personal ponderings, struggles, strategies, and solutions for child rearing. His anecdotes are delightful and clear illustrations of the creativity and patience that successful parenting demands and of how Tom has found ways to succeed. Because of who I am, there's a lot in here that grabs me, including the Caboose Rule, Start the Conversation Over, Coaching Is a Privilege, and Any Game / Any Time; and most of chapter 3, Manners Matters—lots of slaps on my wrist coming up!

Tom Sturges is living proof that the dedication of mind, time, and energy can be marvelously rewarded. From what I have seen, there is no bigger commitment in life than dedicated parenting, and there is no more powerful a reward than the deep, unique happiness that comes from the love of one's children. This reward comes just as much from the immediate smiles, trust, and the warm melting of their bodies into ours for comfort as it does from knowing that we have successfully launched our children into adulthood while giving them the certainty that we will be forever watching with loving hearts.

The approach Tom lays out for us in *Parking Lot Rules* is not an easy one. For many reasons, not all parents can or do show such dedication to the active raising of their children. Yet it is always a blessing to learn something new from another person that improves your spirit, your set of parenting tools, or anything else about your life. In *Parking Lot Rules*, Tom Sturges shares a tremendous variety of gems. He shares them in such an interesting and articulate way that it is hard to imagine any reader putting this book down without having gained something valuable from it.

Contents

Contents

Introduction

Sixteen years ago, when my son Thomas was born, Antonina, his mother, and I were suddenly thrust into a role for which we had no training, no experience, no expertise, no real knowledge, and, really, nowhere to go to get it.

We were . . . parents?

Sure, I had hung out with lots of other people's children, but it is a whole different game when you are suddenly 100 percent, completely responsible for another human being. As I stared lovingly at the complete stranger in my arms, who was busy squawking his little head off, it occurred to me that I did not know a thing about raising him.

Absolutely nothing.

It is harder to get a driver's license than it is to become a parent. With a license, at least you get a pamphlet to leaf through before the big test. Not so with parenting.

There were more self-help books than help-your-children books. There were more dependable guides about walking through Europe than there were dependable guidelines for taking the right steps as the kind of dad I wanted to be. There were books about getting pregnant, naming your zygote, what to eat during the fifth month, the value of listening to Mozart during the third trimester, all that kind of thing. There were books on throwing children's parties and inspiring young minds with arts and crafts and hanging mobiles, some good books on coaching baseball and soccer and dealing with an angry teen.

But I did not want just to be a dad: I wanted to be the greatest father that there had ever been. I wanted my children to be talking about me their whole lives, and how great it was to have me for their dad. I wanted to be the John Wooden of parents. It was all about the legacy for me, from the first moment I looked Thomas in the eye.

But how do you teach a child to be kind and honest, insightful and inquisitive, athletic, curious, loving and gracious, thoughtful . . . ? How do you give a child a huge heart, an understanding of loyalty, and the courage it takes to be a good sport, a good brother, and a good son? Where do you even find the book that teaches you how to teach him?

There were books, but none that spoke to me about the real tasks ahead: Being a parent. Raising a child.

I wanted to be so much more than a casual observer of his life as it went by me. I wanted to be the gardener of his soul. Unfortunately, there were no tools in the shed. No sharp blade to till the soft soil of his endless potential, no pail of kind water to nourish the seeds of hope I planned to plant in his heart, no rake to gather the fallen leaves of his life's disappointments, no compass to direct where to lay out his big dreams.

I had plenty of passion but no knowledge, a great wish list of things to do with him and for him, but no wisdom of how to put any of them into practice. I had will, but not way.

So I started to come up with my own ideas and guidelines for raising Thomas. I would overhear an occasional nugget of wisdom spoken by a complete stranger. I would speak to other parents about their adventures in parenting, and ask if they had anything they could share with me. I never assumed I was always right in what I did, and was open to every suggestion that was made to me. I always tried to imagine how the child must feel in any given situation. I would always try to take into consideration just how much bigger we were than he was, and how that must impact any conversation or interaction between parent and child.

After many stops and starts, I began to write down the ideas that worked best. I kept notes on my parenting, carefully identifying those ideas that were good, and why, as well as those that were not so good, and why not. A trend began to emerge. Every idea that *did* work utilized some aspect of patience, respect, tenderness, caring, encouragement, inspiring, passion, listening, trying harder, never giving up, and always putting the child first.

Ideas that did *not* work were also plentiful, unfortunately. These included Darkroom Baths, Child Steers While Daddy Drives, and probably the worst idea ever: Downhill Tricycle Drag Races (aka, Time Trials), in which boys speed down a steep hill into a huge pile of trash cans while trying to catch a tennis ball thrown at them by yours truly. How Many Peas Fit in an Ear (a counting game) was such a bad idea it is hardly worth mentioning.

But the *good* ideas became rules for Thomas to live by, and for us, his parents, to live by while we were raising him. This was the beginning of the Parking Lot Rules.

I imagined that the Rules would be like guardrails on a bridge. He might not ever need them, but it was good for him to know they were there. These were rules that protected and defended him, rules that guided and mentored him. The Rules brought a mantle of respect into every day of his life. They could help him better understand the complex and challenging world in which he was growing up.

The early ones were easy, and logical. Stand next to me in a parking lot (Parking Lot Rules). Your Child Has to Know Where You Are (when out shopping, for instance; not the other way around). Wear a brightly colored and numbered jersey when we travel (the John Elway Rule). No Reason to Hit—Ever and the No-Yelling rules were, of course, naturals. The Four Best Times to Wash Hands and No Hands to the Face (the Bon Jovi Rule) helped him avoid many colds and sick days out of school.

Soon we needed rules to play by. The Tap-Tap Rule (how to quickly and immediately stop *any* game), the ESPN Rule (how to tell a story about a child's accomplishments to others), and the Game Day / Next Day rule (how to treat a child athlete on the day of the contest) proved to be very effective. Coaching Is a Privilege was inspired by a friend who quit baseball because of a mean-spirited Little League coach.

With all the sports and all the playing, there were all the little injuries that children endure when they are having lots of fun. Take the Pain Away, Freeze It / Then Clean It, and Slow-Motion Replays soon found a place in Thomas's life. Thomas was never the one weeping on the sidelines during a tough game.

As Thomas got older, things of course changed. Disciplines and Punishments became necessary elements in his world, and new rules were created to allow for them. The Truth Reduces the Punishment by 90 Percent was the first. The Ten-Second Rule (how long a parent should wait before saying *anything*) and Five Very Effective Nonviolent Punishments also fit very well. When Sam arrived—the other greatest thing that ever happened to me, about six years later—the Rules required more flexibility, to allow room for two boys in the equation, not just one. Kids Court, The Five Best Times to Talk to Your Child, Smile When You See Them, Start the Conversation Over—each of these ensured that both boys were playing on the same level field, in spite of the six years' difference in their age, intellect, and physical prowess.

Sam also brought with him different challenges, and different rules were required. It turned out that he was much more sensitive than his brother to criticism and praise, and my inability to recognize this trait inspired the rules Lyric and Melody as well as Treat Her Like Your Boss, and the Yes-Not-What rule.

The more I loved these boys, the more I got out of loving them; the more I parented them, the more I got out of parenting them. The more I gave, the more I got. The better I was able to make their childhood, the better I started to feel about my own.

It occurred to me then, and the idea has never left me, that if I could raise my children right, it would heal me. If you can raise your children right, it will heal you, too.

This point was made particularly clear to me when Thomas was about to be three years, two months, and one week old, exactly the age I was when my father died, the day everything changed, the day I lost my way and did not even know it.

I had carefully marked the calendar, and counted down, and then when we were having lunch on the actual day, I said, "Thomas, this is a very important day for Daddy-boy." He looked up at me earnestly and said, "Dad, can I ask you a question?" I looked at him lovingly and replied, "Of course, of course. What is it, Son?" He bit his lip with great sincerity and looked me right in the eye. "Dad, can I have another cookie?"

The rest of the day passed like any other, but somehow everything had changed and everything was different. I felt a weight had been lifted from me, like a bar taken off my heart, like watching silent lightning flash across a distant sky. I realized that I was as innocent and helpless the day my father died as my Thomas was asking me for the cookie. He could not know what was going on, and I realized that, way back then, neither did I. Daddy's Gone to Heaven was almost the same as Daddy's Gone to Ralph's.

That day I forgave myself for losing my dad.

I felt a deep scar inside me heal just a little bit, and I discovered, quite by accident, that by loving my children I could recover my own lost childhood.

Now that both my sons are a little older, I can see how well the Rules have worked and influenced their lives, enabling them to know what to do and when to do it in almost any circumstance.

They are both amazing children and inspire my parenting.

This is not to say they are perfect. A few days ago Thomas and I were sitting next to each other at one of the big family dinners. He was upset that I used his cellphone without asking and was more than a little rude in the way he told me. I asked him to please excuse himself from the table and meet me in the kitchen.

Very respectfully, quietly, and without embarrassing him, I let him know this was not how sons speak to their fathers. Even though it was just the two of us, I whispered it to him. I also reminded him that I was imparting this news in the most respectful way I knew how. He agreed that he was in the wrong and thanked me for not embarrassing him in front of the rest of the family. We returned to the table, rejoined the dinner, and said no more about it.

This moment with Thomas illustrates the most basic premise of the Parking Lot Rules. It is impossible to show a child too much respect, but it is worth the effort to try. Showing respect must be the first and most important ingredient when facing any situation where children are involved.

There is no one way to raise children. Each one of them is a unique gift, with remarkably individual needs and wishes and hopes and dreams. Meanwhile, parenting is a real-time event, very much in the here and now. It requires flexibility and insight, and wisdom not yet gained, and the awareness of when to say just the right thing and when to say absolutely nothing.

Guidance is hard to come by, and my hope is that parents who are committed to raising amazing children will find in these pages a range of options to choose from when it comes to their most precious creations, their children, and the most gratifying experience they will ever know, parenting those children.

These are the Parking Lot Rules.

Chapter 1
EVERY DAY

PARENTING IS A FULL-TIME, twenty-four-hour-a-day collection of duties, obligations, privileges, and promises. It is a series of steps we take every day to protect, defend, educate, nurture, sympathize with, mentor, feed, drive around, cheer for, and provide whatever else is needed for our children at any particular moment.

Our children, in turn, agree to let us do these many things for them. The relationship between us and our children is not equal, and not necessarily balanced, either.

Our first responsibility as parents is to get our children through each and every day of their lives healthy and happy and confident in the fairness of the world around them.

Here are some ideas to keep your children safe, healthy, respected, and cherished, every single day.

PARKING LOT RULES

In a world inhabited by cars the size of small houses, the parking lot can be an incredibly dangerous place. Children are often distracted and unaware of the chaos going on around them—the dangers of getting from the car to the store and back.

The drivers of the SUVs rumbling by are likewise in another world: watching their own children, talking on their cellphones, listening to the radio, organizing for their next stop, just as you are probably doing. Will they triple-check the rearview mirror as they back out? You hope so, but maybe not. The last thing they are looking for is your children.

Teach your children Parking Lot Rules, that they need to be *right next to you* always and whenever you are in a parking lot. There is to be no trailing behind. No racing ahead. No exceptions. Right next to you.

The moment you near a parking lot, either to or from the car, call out "Parking Lot Rules" and your children will know that they absolutely *must* be by your side. If they have toys in their hands, or Game Boys, or PSPs, or (if you're lucky) a good book, it gets put away that instant.

Nothing is more important than their walking next to you, holding your hand, and safely getting back and forth from the car.

This rule can apply in other situations as well. There will be times when you perceive a danger that your children have missed: perhaps raised voices or the sound of broken glass or a stranger acting erratically. If you call out to your children to watch out for the danger, you simply call more attention to yourself and the vulnerability of your situation.

Instead shout out "Parking Lot Rules." Your children will know instantly and instinctively that they need to be by your side, that instant, no questions asked.

FINGERS FINGERS

Getting in and out of the car—which happens a million times during childhood—can be dangerous for children if they are not paying attention, and especially as the car door is closing. This is often the precise instant that they reach for you, or push their sister, or drop a toy and go to rescue it.

As you are about to close the door, call out "Fingers fingers," and teach your children that this means that they should pull their hands back instantly, and protect their fingers.

Your children will soon become accustomed to heeding your warning and will instinctively protect themselves and their beautiful hands. This rule will also remind you to take one last look before you shut the car door.

There is no feeling worse than closing a car door on fingers, whether your children's or someone else's.

Once the injury starts to heal up—and the bruises fade, and the cast comes off, and the new nail grows in—you will have to suffer through the retelling of the story for exactly as long as the rest of your life. It will become a milestone of their childhood, and a millstone of your parenting.

A little warning can make all the difference and give your children that extra second that they just might need to pull fingers out of danger.

GROW THE TREE YOU GOT

Imagine that there is a tree growing in a front yard somewhere. Imagine that it is a tree born of one of the most magnificent oak tree strains in the world, the Kentucky black oak. But then imagine that the man who owns this particular house does not care for the beautiful oak. He always wanted an Australian acacia growing in his front yard.

So he does not appreciate the amazing tree. He hardly notices how it shoots into the sky, filling the air with the musky scent of amber and coal. He does not see its branches seeking the freedom of the clouds. He does not know and does not care that its massive roots feed younger and smaller trees nearby.

When the oak fails to yield the occasional purple blooms that the acacia would have given, he is dismissive of the shade it provides. When the wind blowing through the leaves of the oak does not whistle the susurrus of the acacia that he remembers from his youth, he stands deaf to the birds who twitter as they make their home in the oak's wide branches. When the oak scrapes the front of his house trying to survive a vicious windstorm he is unforgiving and cuts off the branch.

The oak cannot do enough to please the man, and soon the man does not even see the magnificent tree when he comes home. There is a gift waiting for him in his front yard every single day but he does not notice it.

What has this to do with the raising of amazing children?

Parents often visualize a whole scenario of activities that will take place when their children finally arrive. Two very dear friends of mine were no different in this regard.

Edgar and Sonya had tried for many years to have children. Every attempt brought more expectations, and every failure somehow doubled those expectations. Finally they were rewarded with a son. Patrick was several weeks early, but survived to become a healthy young man.

My friends pictured Patrick as an athletic boy, given to prowess in any sport to which he set his mind, with great hand-eye coordination. He was sure to be the high school jock his dad had almost become. From the earliest days his room was filled with balls and bats, while posters of his father's sports heroes fought for wall space next to Barney, Rugrats, and Teletubbies.

The weight of the parents' dreams must have been overwhelming for Patrick. Although he did try soccer and baseball for one season each, it turned out that he was not very athletic. Patrick could not throw or kick a ball and could not have cared less.

By the time he was eleven, Patrick was going out of his way to avoid any discussion about sports. If it involved a ball or bat or glove or puck, he wanted no part of it.

Pretty soon the only sound you could hear around the house, at least when the talk turned to athletics, was the father looking at his son and letting out a long and noticeable sigh. Patrick was forced to wear this mantle of failure, especially around his father.

As a result, father and son never had a chance to become friends. To this day they maintain a polite but very distant relationship.

Patrick's dad had his heart set on raising an Olympian, and so missed out on raising the painter and storyteller his son turned out to be.

If there is a lesson here for parents, it is that we must recognize the innate gifts and individual talents that each child possesses. We must separate our own expectations from those of our children and give them a great life based on who and what they are, not who or what we had always hoped they would be.

Oak, acacia, redwood, or pine. Athlete, dancer, artist, or scholar.

Grow the tree you got.

SMILE WHEN YOU SEE THEM
The Nancy Armato Rule

Antonina's mother, Nancy Armato, is the ultimate child greeter. She smiles and beams and bursts with pride at the sight of her three children and her six grandchildren. No child who enters her home has any doubt whatsoever that he or she is completely welcome—there is no room for doubt.

Grandma Nancy's hugs, kisses, compliments, questions about a new toy or shoes, recognition of a sterling report card, or her recalling a goal in a recent soccer game—all are part of her fabulous greeting. Every child gets his moment.

The children around her respond in kind. They feel so loved and welcomed by her that it literally and physically changes them. They open to her like roses bathed in the warmth of the morning sun. She adds a patina of grace to their lives when each one realizes they have given her reason to smile.

Watch your son walk into a room. What is the first thing he does?

He looks around at the faces watching him walk in. He is instinctively searching for the visual cues that tell him that he is welcome and a part of the family, that he is loved and wanted, and that he was missed while he was gone.

9

The easiest and simplest way to give him the approval and welcome he seeks is to smile when you see him. A smile instantly sets him at ease. A smile says, "Yes, I love you."

A frown, or only a grunt of recognition, faint praise, or sheer disinterest, sends a message of dismissal.

Let your son feel welcome from the first moment he sees you. Let him know that he is loved and important to you, always and forever. When you see him, smile, and leave no doubt that at that moment he is the most important person in your world.

ONCE SEEN, NEVER UNSEEN

When I was only nine years old, and living with my mom and my brother in the Hollywood Hills of California, our traditional Sunday dinner was interrupted by the sound of screeching tires and a huge explosion.

We raced outside to see that two cars had collided head-on in the middle of Franklin Avenue. Hubcaps were still spinning on the pavement as we ran over to see if we could help. A fire was just starting in the Volkswagen, and the other car was on its roof. My mom was five feet, five inches tall and weighed a hundred pounds at the most, but she somehow found the strength to pull the passenger, a six-two man, out of the burning VW and drag him twenty feet away, where she ministered to him until the police and fire and ambulances finally came.

But the driver of the VW was not so lucky. I guess he had banged his head pretty hard and was nearly unconscious. When I walked up to ask him if he was okay, I looked inside the car. His feet were on fire. A minute later, the whole thing burst into a big flame and he disappeared in it. I could not take my eyes off him. Now, of course, I wish I had.

Once seen, never unseen. The images that seared across my retinas that night so many years ago are with me today and will be with me forever. My mother would tell you that she told me not to look, but how could I not?

Today, when I am watching television with my boys, I am overwhelmed by the images that have become so commonplace. It's not just the news or the spectacle stations, but all the crime show ads and Court TV and CNN.

In films, on television, in the newspaper, on the Internet, in everyday life, disturbing visuals are everywhere. Protect your little people from sad sights that will stay with them forever. Cover their eyes if they are too young to do it themselves, and teach them to cover their own eyes as soon as they can. There is no good reason for your child to know the morbid details of the passings and the horrors that are captured and broadcast these days.

Once seen, never unseen.

TREAT HER LIKE YOUR BOSS

No matter how tired or fed up you are with how things are going at the office or store or school, or wherever you might work, if the person who signs your paycheck walks in, somehow there is a little reserve of goodwill saved up, just for him or her.

From out of thin air comes a smile or a sudden lilt in the voice, or a very optimistic assessment of the absolute disaster staring everyone in the face. This good-natured version of you is like a can of emergency survival instinct, always there somewhere, just waiting to be used.

This is the source to which you might consider turning when you are completely fed up with your daughter, when she has found your last nerve and is standing on it, when you realize you have memorized the phone number of the private military academy over in the next county.

But instead of raising your voice to her, instead of saying some things you may regret later, instead of reminding her that you brought her into this world, instead of embarrassing her in front of the entire family, even though that is precisely what she deserves, just imagine . . .

What would you do if your boss suddenly walked into the room? Hmmm. Would you pull him by the earlobe? Would you stick your finger in his face and hiss like a snake? Would you ask

13

him the same question over and over? Would you ask him the same question over and over? Would you call him a name? Would you call him by his full name in a loud voice with lots of extra pronunciation on all the consonants?

Probably not. Not if you wanted to keep your job.

To your boss you would show complete respect and consideration. To your boss you would give the benefit of the doubt. There is no concession you could not make, and no compromise that could not be reached.

Your daughter should get the same respect, if not more. Why not let her meet the kind and considerate you hiding there behind the angry and frustrated version? Why not introduce her to the resilient spirit who always finds a reason to laugh at a situation, regardless of how dire?

Let her say hello to the forgiving optimist who makes a self-deprecating remark to lighten the mood, and makes the whole room laugh. Let her hang out with the practical gamer who always finds a way to look at the bright side of things.

Treat her like your boss.

ALMOST ALWAYS SKIP THE FIRST THING THAT COMES TO MIND

I was playing golf with my son Sam in Los Angeles. He was a pretty good golfer for a six-year-old but was not really concentrating this particular day and topped the ball three times in a row. "Topped" means that the bottom of the club hits just the very top of the ball, moving it forward only a few feet. He must have known that I would be unhappy with his poor play, and looked up at me just to get the confirmation.

I was surprised by how many things I thought of to say to him, none of which was very nice. For instance, that he was not going to Stanford if he kept playing like that. That he was not going to win the 2020 Masters if he did not start concentrating. And on and on.

But instead, I skipped over all the first things that came to mind. Finally I said to him, "Must have been a tough lie, Sam. Keep trying, okay?" He was so relieved that I was not upset with him, his courage visibly blossomed.

He grabbed his three-wood and walked over to his ball. He set up his shot and hit the ball perfectly—a hundred yards down the middle of the fairway. For the rest of the day his game was back on track and we shared a great afternoon.

By saying nothing, I said so many things. By avoiding the obvi-ous negative, I offered him hidden and unexpected positives. By saying nothing bad, I said that everything was good, especially between us.

As parents, when we see our children falter, so often the first thing that comes to mind is a harsh or judgmental comment. Meanwhile, the child is at his most vulnerable. The words we say—no matter how we say them—will be amplified and under-scored.

A careless remark can leave a mark that lasts a lifetime. Un-less your comment is kind and generous, supportive and under-standing, it is almost always best to skip the first thing that comes to mind.

8

FIVE LITTLE PHILOSOPHIES

A philosophy for living can be a great asset, especially for a child. It is a tool that he or she can come to rely on when dealing with the stresses of everyday living. A good philosophy can help children find strength and courage when they need it most.

Children are faced with so many awkward and stressful situations in a day. There are many moments of minor crisis, whether it is maneuvering to avoid friction with a sibling or a parent, struggling to get good grades, vying for a place on a sports team, doubting popularity, being fearful of a bully, or wondering what will happen after they die. They are, frankly, buffeted by life.

Maybe you have already introduced simple philosophies such as "do unto others" or "try, try again."

They are tried and true, yes, but not as complex as might be called for in these often troublesome and fast-moving times.

Here are five little philosophies that can guide your son or daughter to a positive and winning day from the moment he or she wakes up until the second his or her head hits the pillow that night:

MAYA ANGELOU—Maya Angelou is one of the most gifted thinkers and poets America has ever produced. Her approach is simple and straightforward and very honest. She makes complex emotional issues easier to understand. My favorite of her many philosophies is "The past is the past and the future is perfect." Children live in a world with often judgmental and insensitive peers. They must compete for each moment of dignity and respect they will receive. Let your sons and daughters come to believe that every day is another chance to start all over again.

QUINCY JONES—Gifted genius, artist, musician, composer, arranger, producer, executive, and legend, Quincy is a thankful and gracious man who appreciates every moment on earth.

His approach to living is summed up in this philosophy: "Every day you see the grass from above is another beautiful day." Let your child come to know this simple appreciation of the basic joy of just being here.

SICILIAN FISH—There is much practical wisdom that comes from the island of Sicily. This is a culture that reveres respect and honor. One of the most relevant of many amazing Sicilian aphorisms is "A fish dies with its mouth open."

What does this mean? Think for a moment about your life and what has gotten you into the most trouble. What has caused you to make more apologies than anything else? What has created more misunderstandings? What has injured the pride of more friends, or possibly even cost you a romance?

More than likely it was not your arms or hands or feet. Not your eyes or your ears. Not your style or your sassy. No, it was your mouth. Words once said can never be unsaid. Words once heard are never unheard.

Teach your children that one thing they can do to avoid more heartache and inspire fewer apologies is to just keep the mouth shut. When in doubt, think "Sicilian Fish."

BAD NEWS FIRST—Nothing is worse for a parent than bad news undelivered.

How can we react, defend, protect, or rescue our children if we do not know what has happened to them? Whether it is poor grades, a relentless bully, a harsh teacher, a disrespecting coach, even a broken heart, or the sad tale of a candy bar pilfered in an unexplainable moment of weakness, teach children to share the bad news first.

You can only deal with a problem if you know that it exists.

A MOMENT OF HAPPINESS—There are a few moments in every day when you realize that you are doing exactly what you want to do with exactly the people you want to be with. You might be alone, enjoying a cup of coffee with the morning paper, or in a car full of children on the way to the movies. You might be with a complete stranger who has stopped to help when your car ran out of gas in the rain, or sharing a secret with a lifelong friend from whom you keep no secrets.

These are all moments of happiness. Teach your children to recognize and welcome the little bloom of euphoria that accompanies one, when everything is just right, when they are doing exactly what they want to do with exactly the people they want to be with.

MAKE LIFE PROMISES
AND KEEP THEM

It should forever be a goal that children trust their parents. They *must* be able to trust their parents, or there is no future. If there were a children's bill of rights, the right to trust parents would be first.

Children want to believe that they can rely on their parents, in times of difficulty as well as in times of plenty. They want to believe that their parents will support them and encourage them, even if their parents do not agree with all of their choices. They want to believe that they can trust their parents to look out for them no matter how dire or awkward or unfortunate a circumstance has become.

But how do we inspire them to believe and trust in us? And once they do, how do we nurture and prolong and preserve that trust? These are excellent questions.

One way to develop a lasting trust with your son or daughter is to tell him or her the truth on a regular basis. By being true to your word and, most important, doing what you say you are going to do, you will win them over, bit by bit and day by day.

Do this by making "Life Promises," and then keeping those

promises. A Life Promise is a big promise that you keep for the rest of your life. Not only because it is the right thing to do, but because it will demonstrate to your child that you can keep a promise for your whole life.

This simple mechanism of expectation and delivery will let your child begin to understand that you talk the talk and walk the walk, that when you say you are going to do something, you do it. And when you say you are not going to do something, you do *not* do it.

The making and keeping of Life Promises will start to develop a strong and lasting bridge of trust between you and your son or daughter. If you make a big promise to your daughter when she is very young, and you keep that promise every day of her life, she will trust in you: She cannot help but trust in you. She will have no reason not to believe what you say.

As an example, I have made four Life Promises to Thomas:

1. I will never hit him.
2. I will never yell at him.
3. I will never scare him.
4. I will never embarrass him in front of his friends, particularly girls.

I know what the promises are, and he knows what they are. Keeping them is a part of my life with him. He has to be able to trust me, and this is one way of proving to him that I am deserving and worthy of his trust.

This idea arrived one night when I was staring long and hard into Thomas's future, realizing that there could come a day when he might get himself into trouble and not know how to get out of it. A day might arrive when he needs someone he can trust completely.

How could I teach him that he could trust me, and trust *in* me, and turn to me at that sad moment? If I have kept my Life Promises to him for his entire life, when I tell him to trust that I will be able to help him, he should believe me. He would know in his heart that I would do everything in my power to keep that new promise, too, just as I kept the old ones.

It is like a savings account of trust. I deposit a little something into it every day, and it will be there when it is needed. That's the plan, anyway.

The making and keeping of Life Promises is one of the foundational elements of my relationship with both my sons. I treasure the trust that I have saved up.

A world without trust is a prison for the heart. A child who never learns to trust will never learn to love or be loved. Trusting and loving are linked to each other like birds and sky, like tree and land, like dolphin and ocean, like parent and child. They are better for each other when they are together.

Make Life Promises and keep them. Inspire your daughters and sons to trust you and trust *in* you for their entire lives.

10

EVERY DAY STAY HEALTHY
Techniques to Avoid the Common Cold

Do everything possible to avoid catching colds, even if it is a little embarrassing at times. Let the germs pass you and your family by. Here are some ways how:

1. WASH HANDS. WASH HANDS. WASH HANDS.

   A *Parents* magazine study in 2006 concluded that the number one way children get sick is via the transfer of germs from unclean hands into their vulnerable bodies. Keeping hands clean is the easiest and simplest way to protect children from easily preventable sickness and infection.

2. PROTECT THE SOFT PALATE AND GARGLE THE GERMS AWAY.

   The soft palate is one of the first places where germs find refuge in your child's body. It is a landing zone for infection from hands, toys, and the airborne germs that visit with every breath. During cold and flu season, have your child gargle with a gentle mixture of mouthwash and water. He can do this right after brushing his teeth. Have him tip his head back as far as it can go, stick his tongue out as far as he can get it, and say aaaaahhh as long as he possibly can. Rinse and repeat and avoid swallowing!

3. NO SICK FRIENDS.

When your daughter's best friend shows up for a play date or a hangout after school, and she has a runny nose and red eyes, or a cough and a sniffle, just send her home. No need to be impolite or uncivil, but thank her for coming over, invite her to come back when she is feeling better, and shut the door. If this seems harsh or unkind, give her a cookie. If it is your daughter who is not feeling well, show the same respect and keep her away from other children until she is feeling healthy again.

4. NO EXTRA MUCUS.

The extra mucus that shows up at the very beginning of a cold is a sure sign that a cold is looking for a home. Mucus is the body's reaction to inflammation. It is a harbinger of ill health and an enemy of your child's good health. However you can, get it out of your child's body. Blow, cough, spit, snort, tongue-scrape, whatever—just recognize what its presence is telling you, and get rid of it.

11

THE FOUR BEST TIMES
TO WASH HANDS

Establish routine times during the day that will remind your children it is time for them to wash their hands, and over the course of time they will learn to wash their hands on a regular and constant basis. Clean hands will become a habit, and the goal of better health always will be more easily met.

Teach your children these best times to wash hands:

WHEN YOU COME HOME

Make it a rule of the house that all children must wash their hands the very first thing when they walk into the house. If they resist, wash your hands with them—a duet of hand cleanliness. Once your children start washing hands without your gentle reminders, look for their clean hands and nails and compliment them for following the rules so well.

WHEN YOU USE THE BATHROOM

This may seem obvious, but children are children. The bathroom is frequently an interruption of something much more enjoyable. They rush in and rush out. Instruct them from their very earliest days to wash their hands before leaving the bathroom. No exceptions. Some parents might offer extra credit for the child who washes his or her hands both before and after!

Before and After You Eat

For many children, this might be the easiest time for them to remember to wash their hands during the course of their day.

When You Go to Bed

At the end of the day, children often have to get one more "play" in with one or all of their favorite toys. But toys are not the most germ-free items, and these same hands will be rubbing eyes and scratching noses in no time. Make sure that the last thing they do in their day, right before bed, is wash their hands. Clean hands lead the way to healthier sleep, and maybe even better dreams.

12

NO HANDS TO THE FACE
The Bon Jovi Rule

One of the biggest rock bands ever, and one of the most successful and dependable touring groups in the world, is Bon Jovi. Richie Sambora is one of the founding members, and he is also a wonderful and devoted father to his daughter, Ava.

Richie once shared his insights on the unbelievable success the band has achieved. He believes that their ability to stay healthy on the road is one of the keys to the band's impressive longevity.

The band will often bring a nurse, a nutritionist, a cook, and a chiropractor on the road with them when they are out on a world tour. But he said they also follow this rule: No Hands to the Face.

One day's sickness can cost the band a well-planned and well-promoted concert date and completely disrupt their tight touring schedule, which in turn leads to a loss of ticket sales and goodwill, diminished merchandise revenue, and the possibility of developing a reputation for canceling shows. Millions of dollars are at stake every night.

Rock-and-roll stars have to shake so many hands and encounter so many strange new germs during the course of a tour, whether greeting their crew and fans backstage, signing autographs at local record stores, or attending after-parties, not to mention the handles and doorknobs and car seats and money and bathrooms that they come into contact with every day as well.

You will almost never see Richie Sambora sticking his finger in his eye if he's got an itch. Instead he will use a sleeve, a cuff, a shirttail, a tissue, or whatever else is available. Anything but a hand.

Let your children learn how to stay healthy from one of the greatest rock bands in the world. Teach your children the Bon Jovi Rule: No Hands to the Face.

13

WHY GERMS LOVE MONEY

The U.S. Bureau of Printing and Engraving says the average dollar bill has a lifespan of eighteen months. Coins, according to the U.S. Mint, are much longer lasting and can stay in circulation for more than thirty years! Think of the extraordinary number of transactions that take place during the lifetime of coin and paper money. Think about how many hands are touching it to get through those thousands of purchases. Then think how many of those people were sick at the time. *Discover* magazine published an article in 1998 reporting that handling money is one of the most common ways germs travel in our society and are able to reach out and infect our children.

Put these relatively disparate facts together and they point to a most unfortunate conclusion: Money + Children = Nothing Good. And the reason why germs love money.

Germs find easy refuge in the money in our pockets. Built to last, paper currency is actually a very durable piece of cloth. It is woven strands. Where the fabric lines intersect, there are little pockets. These pockets can hold enough germs to give you, your child, and everyone in the household many more colds than you will ever need.

Money travels fast, much faster than we can build up immunities to the germs that live on it. A businessman with a bad cold in New York can infect a child in Los Angeles with only three degrees of separation: He pays a fare to a cabdriver whose next customer is a model going to Kennedy Airport. She arrives in L.A., stops at a Starbucks, and pays with the infected dollar. That same dollar is given in change to a child who forgets to wash his hands after touching the money. The child rubs his eyes on the way to the car and is sniffling and sneezing before he gets home from his violin lesson.

Some studies have shown that certain germs can live up to eighteen hours on a dollar bill.

When your children touch money, wipe their hands clean as soon after as possible. If soap and water are not easily available, brush their hands with your clean hands, or your shirt cuff, an antibacterial towelette, or a product like Purell. Just get the germs off.

Money should never go anywhere near the mouth or face, either. So if your child is one of the millions who like to suck on quarters just for the taste, please put a stop to this immediately.

Chapter 2
COMMUNICATING WITH YOUR CHILDREN

THE MOST IMPORTANT LINK between parents and children is the way they communicate with one another.

Children will learn how to communicate with the world based in large part on how they have learned to communicate with their parents, coaches, mentors, and other elders.

Among the greatest gifts we can give our children are the tools and skills and knowledge that will enable them to exchange ideas with all the rest of us walking around on the planet.

Our children should know how to ask excellent questions and listen to the answers, know how to communicate without words if necessary, know how and when to whisper, and know always to show respect when talking and listening, among other skills.

These are some ideas for communicating with your children and getting the most out of the conversations that you have with them as a result.

#14

YES-NOT-WHAT
The Leslie Bricusse Rule

Leslie Bricusse is a devoted husband and father, and one of the most successful songwriters in the world. In addition to writing several Broadway shows, he wrote the lyrics to the James Bond theme songs "Goldfinger" and "You Only Live Twice," as well as all the songs in *Doctor Dolittle* and *Willie Wonka*, including "Candy Man."

Leslie lives at the center of a busy universe filled with songs and music, lyrics and licenses, samples and reinterpretations of his creations. No matter where he is or what he is doing, people are always calling out his name.

But he is never annoyed by all the noise, the phone always ringing, the requests back and forth, the constant demands for his attention.

He actually seems to revel in the cacophony. He instinctively welcomes everyone who calls out to him. He says: "Yes, my love . . . !" or "Yes, my darling . . . ?" or "Yes, my friend Tom . . ."

By offering this simple greeting, he starts every conversation by showing a sign of respect and appreciation for the person to whom he is speaking.

Leslie is this way with his wife, Eve, and son, Adam, his cowriters and staff, the artists singing his songs, the musicians accompanying him, and all of his employees and business partners. He is a joy to be around for many reasons, but the way he shows his constant respect and welcoming is the one that is most precious to me.

When your daughter calls out to you, answer her Leslie Bricusse–style by saying "Yes?" or "Yes, my love?" or "Yes, my darling?" Or simply answer by saying her name in a loving and respectful way.

Never answer "What?" in response to your daughter calling you. It is unwelcoming and dismissive. It tells her that she has interrupted you, or that you have something more important to do than speak with her. But what could be more important than communicating with your beautiful child?

The question that she is asking you or the dilemma that she has brought to you to solve may seem somewhat insignificant. But to your daughter, this particular request may be a crisis that only you can solve. She chose *you* to solve it.

By responding "Yes, my love?" not "What?" or "What is it?" when she calls out your name, you are reaffirming to her the sweet knowledge that she is one of the most important people in your world.

15

THE EXCELLENT QUESTION GAME

I was driving my son Thomas to baseball practice a few years ago. He was digging around the backseat of the car for change among the cookie crumbs and finally he asked me how much money I thought he had found.

Not intending to be mean or diminishing, I responded, "Well, that's not really an excellent question, is it?" He asked me, "Why not?" I said, "Because you already know the answer. An excellent question would be one where you do *not* know the answer."

We talked the whole drive about questions and what makes them excellent. Once he started to understand what I was after, we started to ask each other excellent questions. Why was the sky blue? How tall was that eucalyptus tree we just passed? How much does a car weigh? What is it like to be a bug? It quickly became a game—who could ask the most excellent question?

The answers became less and less important. They actually seemed to get in the way of the next question. So after a few minutes we decided to skip them entirely.

It was an amazing afternoon, and a tremendous exchange of fresh, beautiful ideas between us.

A few weeks later, at one of the family dinners, I found myself sitting with Thomas and his cousins, Elio and Anthony. I told them that Thomas and I had invented a new game, called the Excellent Question Game. All they had to do to play was ask a question to which they did not know the answer.

After a false start or two, the game began in earnest. As they went around the table, I rated their questions as Okay, Good, Great, or the ultimate, "Excellent question!"

Then they started to ask some amazing questions, some truly excellent questions. Anthony: "How does a tree know to grow up?" Elio: "Who was the first person to walk on the planet?" Thomas: "How much does a cloud weigh?" Anthony: "Where does the sun come from?" Elio: "How do eyes see?" Thomas: "What happens after the stars?"

It was a fantastic moment that unfolded before me, watching their brains work, watching their intellects stretch, watching their minds look for an unknown subject from which another question might spring.

The Excellent Question Game requires only that a child be able to grasp the mere concept of something, and then understand it well enough to discover and develop an excellent question to ask about it. There are no answers. Answers have no value in this game since they only interrupt the search for more excellent questions.

The ability to play the Excellent Question Game can grow into the ability to have a conversation with almost anyone, anywhere, any time. Questions are the best way to get talking started. One question leads to another, and another, and the next thing your child knows, a conversation is taking place.

Resist telling your son or daughter that a question is "difficult" or "tough" or "hard to answer." This only sounds a discouraging note. Instead, marvel at the intellect and the question that it was able to produce.

A child who can discover and create excellent questions will be better prepared to anticipate and challenge the ever-changing world in which he or she will grow up.

16

THE TWENTY-SECOND EXPLANATION

My golf teacher is one of the best athletes and most amazing teachers I have ever met, except for one thing: Mike Perryman cannot give a short answer. He knows too much.

Once, at the beginning of a lesson, I asked him a very simple question about my turn and backswing. Forty-five minutes and several analogies later, he stopped answering. Not because he was finished, but because he had another student waiting.

Mike's depth of understanding of golf and its mechanics was so vast that he could have spoken about my backswing for at least another couple of hours. My cup of knowledge was so small that it was running over shortly after the lesson began.

He lost me at hello.

Mike could not tell me what I wanted to know in just a couple of sentences. He could not give me the *Reader's Digest* edition, the CliffsNotes version, the abbreviated story. And that was what I really needed: a simple and understandable answer that was concise, clear, and easy to remember.

A few days later my son Thomas asked me a question about *his* golf game.

I thought carefully about my answer, remembering the frustration that I was feeling just a few days before. I told him that I could answer his question in twenty seconds if he gave me his total and complete attention for every one of those twenty seconds.

He agreed, but it was clearly going to be a challenge for both of us.

Before I even opened my mouth, I edited and refined and simmered my answer down to its most basic elements—and then counted down the twenty seconds on my fingers while I delivered the answer to him.

It worked. We both won. He got my best answer to his good question and I got his undivided attention while delivering it.

Try not to punish your child for asking good questions. Instead, reward him or her with a simple and understandable answer. If you need a laser pointer, reference books, three trips to the Internet, and at least ten minutes to fashion your response, then you have disrewarded your child for coming to you with a good question.

The Twenty-Second Explanation saves a lot of time.

17

THE IMPORTANCE OF CHILDREN TELLING STORIES AND THE SIGNIFICANCE OF LISTENING TO THEM

Storytelling is a skill that will help your daughter in all aspects of her life.

If she can tell a good story, it gives her greater confidence around her peers and earns her more respect and admiration from her elders. Storytelling helps ease shyness, and lets her be more comfortable when the attention of a room is upon her.

She will be more sure of herself, more confident hearing her own voice. She will be more worldly and wise since she will have become comfortable sharing her stories and wisdom with you. As a result, she will be able to say "no" more readily in those situations where you are not around to guide her.

But to help ensure that your daughter becomes a good storyteller, you must become a good listener. This is the key that unlocks the ability. Good listening inspires good storytelling.

If you show the slightest disinterest or frustration, your daughter will instinctively know and feel it, and this knowledge will change the telling of the story. She will rush to the ending thinking that her time is running out, thinking that her parents want her to stop talking.

You must show incredible patience when listening to your daughter's stories. You must be interested throughout the telling and be surprised by the depth of the knowledge she has to share. Look her right in the eye when she is talking. Say "yes" and "uh-huh" and encourage her to provide lots of details. Ask good follow-up questions and reward her good answers with your praise and laughter.

If a story is tumbling out all over the place, and you are having a hard time following the plot, gently—but very gently—attempt to ask, "Who is this story about, please? What happened to them again? Where did that happen exactly? Why does it matter so much to you, my darling?"

Please do not challenge her knowledge or be suspicious of her sources. Please do not interrupt her to correct the pronunciation of a word that she has used, or to offer a better one. Please do not criticize her choice of subject or the time of day she chose to tell you her story. If she makes a little mistake, leave it alone.

If you judge the story too soon, interrupt and interject, appear upset or miffed, your daughter may think that she is about to get in trouble and change her story, and she will probably think twice before approaching you with another tale of her adventures.

So try to let her tell you the *whole* story before you respond to it. Interrupting a child's storytelling may disrupt some tender wiring, and introduce the possibility of speech and learning difficulties later in her life.

Your daughter can become a great storyteller and share with you all of the stories of her life, if you can understand the significance of the gift you give by simply listening.

#18

THE FIVE BEST TIMES TO TALK TO YOUR CHILD

If your life does not allow you all of the moments that you need to talk with your child, start with these five best times and make the most of the moments that you have:

1. BATH TIME. Absolutely the best time of the day for an exchange of ideas between parent and child is bath time. He is relaxed and comfortable, content and refreshed, and there are few distractions beyond the toys in the tub. Turning off the TV or video games can be very calm and quieting. You can share your wisdom and knowledge, and pay him compliments for good deeds, and plant the seeds of hope and possibility that will become his future.

2. DRIVE TIME. Turn off the radio and video games, shut down the DVD player, and engage your daughter with some drive talkin'. Automobiles are made for good conversation. She is belted in, and all yours, and has nothing else to do until you arrive at your destination. You can bring her into your world by discussing real issues that you are facing in your job, or within the family. It is amazing how often a child's advice is

insightful. Get her suggestions on forthcoming holidays and what the family should do to celebrate. Engage her completely and you will be rewarded with her ideas and wisdom.

3. BEDTIME. The last minutes of the day can also be the most precious of your daughter's day. This is not the time to scold or remind her of the next day's responsibilities. This is the time to be loving and kind, completely supportive and understanding. It is important to be forgiving and let the mistakes of the day go. Allow her heart to be unguarded and her conscience to be clear so that she can sleep in peace.

4. WAKE-UP TIME. This is usually a rushed opportunity in a house filled with people all getting ready to start their days at the same time. But ten minutes of quiet snuggling, encouraging whispers, and gentle waking can set a triumphant tone for any child's day. In the misty half-light between sleep and wakefulness, you can tell her how much you love her, how proud you are to know her, how great this day will be for her. She might not remember every word that you say, but the emotion and power of your words will stay with her all day.

5. ANY TIME HE WANTS. Treasure the rare moment when your child initiates the conversation with you. Treat his questions as though borne on the wings of an exotic butterfly that has come to visit with you. If your son has gotten up the courage or trust, or whatever it is, to find you and have a talk, or ask a question, or seek your advice, honor his choice and give him the next twenty minutes of your life.

19

LYRIC AND MELODY
It's Not Just What You Say, It's How You Say It

Songwriters have always amazed me. Their craft is unique beyond measure. They go into closed rooms outfitted with few tools beyond their hearts and minds, maybe a pencil, their intellect, passions, and some paper. They emerge, some hours or days later, with beautiful, unforgettable melodies chained to remarkable, compelling lyrics.

At its most basic, songwriting is words with melodies, two vastly different art forms that must find peace with each other. From a blending of these two completely separate disciplines, songwriters create emotion and meaning, passion and desperation, in the form of songs that give the rest of us an excuse to fall in love, feel incredible happiness, forgive grudges, fight for our countries, or just fill an afternoon with music.

Imagine that you are a songwriter in your child's life. Your ideas are the lyrics, and how you phrase and shape and present your ideas is the melody and the music. Both lyric and melody must work together to get your message across successfully to your sons and daughters.

I discovered this concept one evening while teaching Sam to read. Regrettably, on this night I got very frustrated with him and it did not go well. So I asked him the same question over and over, and although the words were the same, the message that they delivered was different each time. I learned a lesson that I have never forgotten.

The book was *The Cat in the Hat*. We had devoted several minutes already to recognizing and reading the word *the*. It appears in that book about four million times.

I thought that we had made good progress until we turned a page and came to the next appearance of *the*.

Surprisingly, at least to me, he did not immediately recognize the *the*, at least not as quickly as I thought he should. I said hopefully, "What is that word, Sam?" He said nothing. A pause, then I asked again, in a less gentle, less hopeful voice.

"What is that word . . . Sam?"

My words had not changed, but something else had. It was the melody of those words that was different. The same lyric, but delivered in a diminished tone, the intonation altered, pitched lower. My unguarded frustration was creeping in, and he heard it right away.

"Are you going to be mad at me if I get it wrong?" he asked. It was too late that I noticed his eyes welling up, his lower lip starting to push out.

It was too late that I noticed that there was no melody to go with my lyric, that there was no music in my song. It had become a staccato monotone. I said flatly, "What . . . is . . . that . . . word . . . Sam?" And the dam broke. He burst into desperate tears.

The melody had changed and thus everything had changed. No longer were we in the middle of a lesson in reading that was warm and kind. Instead, he heard a song of warning, a hymn to my disappointment. I had set the bar too high and then given in to my own unreasonable expectations.

I realized instantly and I felt terrible. I begged his forgiveness and dried every tear, at least twice. I made fun of myself for taking it all so seriously. I was not afraid to be completely wrong. Then I made him a "Life Promise": Never ever again would I get upset while I was teaching him something.

Ever since that night I have been so careful about the "songs" that I sing to my boys and all the other children in my life.

The "lyric" is the advice and counsel and wisdom; the "melody" is how the idea is phrased and shaped and presented. A parent never knows which song they sing will end up on the soundtrack of a child's life.

20

YES, IT'S OKAY TO GO OFF-TOPIC

You may find that your beautiful daughter gets a little distracted sometimes. She may not be able to stay on one subject for very long, certainly not as long as you would like. Suppose she just gets bored earlier than most people.

While it is important that she learn to stay on a topic for as long as possible, you must understand that she cannot stay interested as long as you can.

Make every effort to keep the conversation or activity interesting for her, but when she has had enough, teach her to recognize this key turning point, and then teach her how to turn.

Let her know that it is okay to go off-topic, okay to move on to a new subject or a different line of questions, okay to read from a different bedtime storybook, and okay to change things up completely and move to an entirely different activity, *as long as she asks you politely.*

Teach her to recognize when she has lost the plot, and give her a tool to politely let you know, too. She can whisper in your ear, or offer a hand signal that only you will understand. If your child is a little older, you might use an IM, or text message, or even e-mail.

Do not take it personally. Recognize what has happened. Maybe it was a lousy subject to begin with; perhaps you should have simplified your answer. Maybe she does not really care about the difference between stalactites and stalagmites. For whatever reason, you did not keep your daughter interested. You did not keep your customer satisfied.

When he is caught in this conundrum, Sam simply asks me, "May I go off-topic please?" And off we go. He stays interested in being with me, and that, after all, is the only thing that really matters at this stage.

Old Greek saying: Give a man a fish, and he will not be hungry. Teach a man how to fish and he will never be hungry again. New Parking Lot Rule: Change the topic, and your daughter will not be bored for a little while. Teach her how to change the topic and she may never be bored again.

By giving your daughter the ability to recognize when she has lost interest in the topic or the conversation or the activity, and teaching her how to go off-topic with grace and politeness, you will have given her a tool that she can use for the rest of her life.

21

FOUR THINGS YOU CAN SAY
WITH YOUR HANDS

One of the Life Promises I made to Thomas was that I would never do anything to embarrass him, particularly around girls. I have made every effort to keep this promise.

But at the same time, I often want him to know how much I love him, and, frankly, I like to tell him. Unfortunately, boys of a certain age do not want to hug their dads or be overly demonstrative in public. So what to do?

A compromise was obviously required, and it came about when I realized that I could tell him just as easily with my hands as with my voice.

If you ever watch people speak in sign language, you will notice that their hands are extraordinary, graceful like birds, fluttering in stop action, like live anime.

Expressive and gentle when needed, or forceful and argumentative if the conversation takes that turn.

Inspired by their artistry, I learned a few simple signs, and added a couple of my own. They are easy to use and very efficient. They can be clearly seen across a soccer field or at a middle school graduation or over dinner at home. They are:

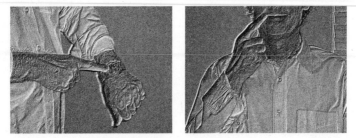

(I'm Having a) Moment of Happiness

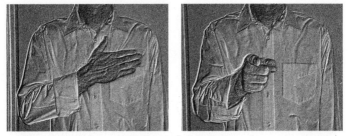

(Daddy Is) Proud of You

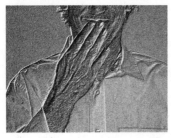

Thank You

I Love You

Design & Photography by Karen Otto

Sign language is one of the most amazing languages ever created. It is the third most widely used language in the United States, according to Handspeak.com. Baby Sign is changing the way parents communicate with their very young children, who can master simple hand signs long before developing control of the complex muscles and systems of speech. To learn more about sign language, go to www.handspeak.com.

Tell your children that you love them and adore them as often as is possible and feasible, but when voices are unavailable or inappropriate, speak with your hands.

22

WHEN YOU GET UPSET, WHISPER

No matter how much you love your children, it is inevitable that you will get upset with them. It happens. Things happen. Children do things that they should not do, often inexplicably, and parents cannot control them.

But parents can control what happens next: the reaction to the thing they did that got you upset in the first place. With all respect to Isaac Newton, and everybody who works in the physics business, every action does *not* have to have an equal and opposite reaction. Just because your angel did something idiotic does not mean that you have to do something idiotic in return.

It is quite natural and normal to be upset, but how you tell them that you are upset makes all the difference.

You (and your voice) are your children's main connection to the rest of the universe. News, weather, travel updates, schedule changes, philosophic and spiritual advice, mentoring and guidance, details of family scandals, episodes from your own childhood—they hear it all from you first. You are Oprah, CNN, NPR, FOX News, the Drudge Report, and the Weather Channel all in one.

You are their everything. It is for this reason that you can never yell at your children.

Yell at your children and it will leave a mark, a scar on their ears and intellect, a forever impression, the memory of your anger as permanent as bright red graffiti on a white picket fence.

They may forget what you said, but they will never forget how you said it.

Children are just like adults—they listen better when they are spoken to in a quiet and respectful manner. Raised voices raise defenses. They will panic when they hear the animosity in your tone. It is instinctive.

Studies show that many children's greatest stress levels are reached when they fear their parents' reactions to something that they have done, and that the anticipation is almost as bad as the reaction they are expecting. So it is likely that they are already acutely aware of the possibility of your anger, and raising your voice is not going to make things any better.

If you really want children to hear every word that you have to say, lean over to them, put your lips close to their ears, and whisper to them. The complete privacy of this interaction and the heat of your breath in their ear will bring full and total attention to every word that you have to say.

Whisper things like "Daddy is very disappointed in the way that you are acting." Or "Mommy does not like it when you treat your sister so unkindly." There is no need to hiss or explode your consonants or in any way sound angry.

Whispering parents inspire; yelling parents intimidate.

There are several other advantages that come with whispering if or when you get upset with your children. Here are five good reasons why it is better to whisper than yell.

Whispering:

- saves your children the embarrassment of being scolded in front of their friends, the family, or worst of all, strangers;
- never gives your children any reason to doubt that you still love them even though you are really upset with them about something they did;
- informs your children respectfully that they were wrong to do what they did, but does not crush their spirit, or embarrass or diminish them;
- makes it easier for your children to listen to you and pay attention, and to learn from what you are telling them;
- never makes you look like you are impatient or unkind or a bully to your children.

While they may be the inspiration for anger, your children should never be the object of anger. Whisper, especially if you are upset.

Whispering can help you gain control of and even defuse your first reaction to a situation, especially if the reaction is charged and emotional.

Your children will know that you have made the choice not to yell at them and will appreciate you all the more for it.

#23

KIDS COURT

I walked into the house one night not long ago and found myself in the middle of complete chaos. There was yelling and crying and boys not talking to each other and tears everywhere.

Once things started to calm down, I was able to gather that Sam and his friend William, who was visiting from England, both five years old at the time, had been playing very well together all day, but now were terribly upset with each other.

Sam was in his bedroom, drying his eyes and crying that snuffling yelp that means that things are almost under control, but not quite. He managed to hiccup out that William had called him a bad name and hurt Sam's feelings terribly.

After a few minutes of searching, I found the sniffling figure of William completely covered by a blanket, sitting all alone in front of the sofa in the living room. I asked the blanket if it was sorry about something that had happened that day. A pause, and then the blanket nodded yes.

I asked the blanket if it wanted to talk about it. After a moment's hesitation, again the blanket nodded, and out came William. He was red faced and sorrowful, and had apparently been crying up quite a storm under there. I hugged him and let him know that I was not angry or upset with him. I just wanted to figure out what had happened.

I took William by the hand and we walked downstairs until we found Sam. Neither boy could look at each other, they were so upset. I found an empty room and sat them down directly opposite each other and closed the door. It was just the three of us.

Very solemnly I looked at both of them. "We are now in Kids Court. Whatever the problem is, it will be resolved between us, here and now. William will speak for two minutes, and then Sam will speak for two minutes. Both of you must listen carefully to what the other has to say. When you are finished, I will make my decision and you both agree to live by it. Okay?" Both boys nodded in agreement. I knew that they both wanted the problem resolved, but they did not know how to resolve it. I reminded them that they were both expected to tell the complete truth, and we began. Testimony quickly revealed that Sam and William were having a pillow fight, which both acknowledged immediately they were not supposed to be having.

In the middle of the unauthorized fracas, Sam caught William with a haymaker that knocked him right off the bed and onto the floor. William retaliated by hitting Sam with a pillow as hard as he could and calling him an idiot and then racing upstairs to hide under the aforementioned blanket.

Apparently the use of the word *idiot* is what got Sam so upset and angry with William.

After some questioning, William admitted that he felt terrible that he had called his friend a name, but he couldn't help himself—sometimes words came out. This confession was accompanied by a rain of tears and regret. Sam corroborated all the details, and admitted again that they should not have been having the pillow fight.

I asked William if he was sorry. He said he was. I asked Sam if he was willing to accept the apology and forgive William. He said he would.

I instructed William and Sam to get close to each other and look each other right in the eye. I grasped their joined hands in mine, paused for a moment, and gave my ruling:

"Kids Court has determined that you boys should not have been having a pillow fight, and that everything that happened afterward was both of your faults equally and that neither boy has legitimate rights in this case for that reason.

"However, Kids Court also discovered that William did call Sam a name. William has apologized for doing that. Sam has accepted his apology. The boys can now be friends again."

And that was it. They shook hands, smiled at each other, and walked away together, their problem completely resolved.

Kids Court is a simple and effective conflict resolution tool whereby children have a chance to hear and be heard, and to present their sides of the story.

You, the parent or mentor or elder, will usually be the judge. You must listen well, ask excellent questions, and get to the truth that hangs somewhere between the two sides of the story that you are being told. Final rulings must be fair and impartial, and give each child something to walk away with. The best verdicts end up somewhere near the middle.

Kids Court can happen any time and anywhere. Sometimes a group of children can hear the evidence collectively and advise the parent or elder what the decision should be. This format works well on car rides, or ski trips, or during Thanksgiving dinner at the children's table.

It is an especially good tool for siblings because it evens the playing field between brothers and sisters of different ages whose communication skills may be vastly different but for whom the conflicts are very real.

Children cannot name-call, or accuse, nor can they respond to the other children's testimony until it is their turn to testify. Taunting or celebrating is absolutely forbidden and can result in an immediate reversal. If a child is in trouble for some other reason not relevant to the case, this fact should not be considered.

Kids Court should be run like a real court. Be incredibly just with your questions as well as your verdicts. Be formal and respectful. Try to nurture in your children a faith in the process so that they learn to trust it and bring their injustices to it again and again.

Kids Court can help develop and discover the truth, and inspire honesty, and gives your children a template to resolve their conflicts in the future when you might not be available to adjudicate.

#24

START THE CONVERSATION OVER

Sam and I were driving home a few weeks ago, talking about desserts and cookies and other very important matters.

We had made an agreement earlier in the evening that he could have *two* cookies for dessert if he promised to take a bath the moment he walked into the house. He had just taken the first bite of the second cookie, and was very pleased with himself, when he let me know that he had no intention of taking a bath—he had just said that to get the second cookie.

With the speed of a mongoose happening upon a nest of snake eggs, I snatched that cookie out of his hand. "What did you just say, Sam?" I asked.

"I was just kidding, Dad, just kidding . . ." he implored.

"I don't think you were. Please tell me why you would say that, or even think of saying something like that." The bottom was dropping out of the good times that we had just been enjoying. Sam gave me one of those looks. "Dad, I can't believe you're getting upset with me about this."

But I could not help it. I did not like that he had been deceptive with me, whether he was kidding or not. Duplicity and disingenuousness are not habits worth pretending or practicing.

But at the same time I did not feel it was *that* big a deal, nor did I feel like ruining our evening together, being his jailer and forcing a punishment on him, even though that was exactly what the situation called for.

So I decided to sidestep the whole mess. I offered him the option of starting the conversation all over again, as though what had just happened had not just happened. As if we were in a scene from *Groundhog Day*. Or sitting with Dick Clark watching a TV bloopers show.

He leaped at the opportunity. I handed him back the cookie. He looked over at me, smiled, and said, "I sure am looking forward to taking that bath when we get home. . . ."

Perfect. The evening was saved and a punishment was avoided, kindly and easily.

Sometimes children may need a second chance. When the infraction is minor, consider the simplicity of starting the conversation over.

#25

THE OTHER SIDE OF THE FREEWAY

Measuring is a big challenge for children. Even simple concepts like height and weight require the use of abstract thought. And what the heck is abstract thought, anyway, to a seven-year-old?

Volume, depth, and distance. Diameter, temperature, and speed. Mass and density. All of these are measurements that require a great imagination as well as a solid working knowledge of physics, *plus* the ability to reason and deduce like a Rhodes Scholar.

Yet we hope our children understand when we use these same concepts to explain the simplest yet most important measurements they need to make in their lives: how much we love them; how much they mean to us; how empty our lives would be without them; and so on. How much is everything, after all?

A mommy can ask her son, "Do you know how much I love you?" His answer might be, "I don't know, but I hope it's a lot." But will the son ever really comprehend how completely his mother loves him?

How can we teach children to measure the unmeasurable, to touch the intangible, to understand the meaning of loyalty and the dream of family? How can we make a son or daughter recognize and quantify passion and commitment, and learn to weigh the strength of his or her own beliefs? I had wondered about this for years until a solution presented itself one day, out of the blue.

They tell us that the I-10 freeway, in Los Angeles, is the busiest freeway in the world. Forty million cars travel on it every year (or something equally remarkable).

Last July, Sam and I were driving on it, westbound toward the ocean, going from one of his summer adventures to the next one, joyfully discussing the details of what had just happened and what was about to happen next, namely a sleepover at a friend's house. At that particular moment, the I-10 West was a freeway designer's dream: blue skies, traffic zipping along at maximum speed, very few cars to get in anybody's way, just perfect . . .

Then I noticed what had just unfolded on the other side of the busiest freeway in the world, the I-10 East. Apparently a truck had jackknifed and deposited in raw fruit the equivalent of forty thousand orange/watermelon smoothies all over those well-traveled lanes. Traffic was so backed up it looked like a still-life painting of a freeway. Not one car was moving.

It was hot, too, and muggy. Not quite Saharan Africa hot, but close. The air was thick and smoggy. I would not have been surprised if a huge silver train had come racing down the carpool lane to the strains of "Love Train" by the O'Jays. It was that hot.

Knowing that I was now going to be very late for an appointment back at the office, I sighed and leaned over to my Sam. "You see that mess over there? I have to drive back in all that—just to get back to the office." He looked over at the backed-up freeway and said, "I'm so sorry, Dad. You don't have to take me."

And suddenly there it was: Out of nowhere I saw an opportunity to show him something that I had been trying to show him for years. I realized right then that I could provide him with a tangible version of something intangible, a chance to see the unseen, like a sculpture of an emotion, or a drawing of a taste. I was finally going to be able to show him a physical representation of how much I loved him.

I told him that I did not mind at all having to sit in all that traffic. That I would be happy to sacrifice a few minutes out of my day, or any day, if it would enable him to have more happiness in *his* day. I smiled and said he could measure my love for him by looking at *all* those stopped cars.

I could almost hear the tumblers spinning in his head until they finally clicked into a sequence that opened a door to a vault and let him see—actually see with his own eyes—just how much I loved him. There it was, right next to him, on the other side of the freeway. All those cars were like little weights on a scale, adding up to an uncountable and unquantifiable mass of evidence of an unstoppable and endless supply.

My willingness to sit in stopped traffic on a paralyzed freeway just so he could have an amazing day was somehow a reverse image, a visible, physical representation of a completely invisible and intangible emotion. The other side of the freeway was how much I loved him.

Once children understand how to measure good things, like love and happiness and your eternal wish for them to have great lives, it is just as important for them to learn how to measure the not-so-good things, like how disappointed you are with their behavior, or how momentarily upset you may be with them for something they did.

One Saturday afternoon, when Thomas was five years old, we were working on a Hooked on Phonics program. The lessons are printed on heavy card stock that is built to last, and meant to be used by many children. When he finished reading the story and doing the exercises, Thomas tossed the card to me.

I was not expecting him to throw it, and I didn't get my hands up in time. The corner of the card hit me right in the face, about a quarter inch from the corner of my left eye. My emotions raced, my anger surged, my adrenaline peaked, and I gritted my teeth and followed as many rules as I could remember.

I did not say the first thing that came to mind. I did not say anything for ten seconds. I did not raise my voice. When I dabbed the spot of blood from my face, I looked over at him and whispered, "If I was a hitting daddy, I would be hitting you right now." This may not have been the kindest way to say it, but those were the words I chose.

Thomas took a sharp intake of breath and burst into tears. Who wouldn't? I am quite sure it scared the jinkies out of him, those words, whispered softly like that. I let it all sink in for a moment, then took him into my arms and tried to console him. I spoke very sweetly and let him know we were both very lucky, and that it could have been a much worse day.

But all of my entreaties met with very little success. Maybe he was crying so hard because he was a little scared, and maybe it was a little bit of a defense mechanism. I finally asked him what exactly was inspiring this river of tears. Between gasped breaths he wailed, "Because you're *so* upset with me . . ." I had whispered one little sentence, and it was abundantly clear that the point was understood—so now what? How could I let him know it wasn't that big a deal, relatively speaking?

Still holding him in my arms, I reached into my pocket and pulled out a quarter and threw it on the floor next to us. I said to him, "Thomas. If this whole room is how much I love you, that quarter is how much I am upset with you for nailing me with the card."

He looked down at the quarter and then back up at my face to see if I was kidding or not. He said, "Really?" When I nodded, he stopped crying. "Well, if that's all it is, I can deal with that much upset-ness." He dried his tears, smiled at me, and told me he loved me and that he was terribly sorry about the whole throwing-of-the-card thing. We got on with the rest of our day and raced off to the movies.

The quarter enabled him to "see" how upset I was, especially when he could compare it to "seeing" how much I loved him. He had context and could give relative value to the two emotions that were in play at that moment: my love for him, and my displeasure with him.

One of our many challenges as parents and mentors, coaches and teachers, is to show all the children in our lives how much we love and respect them, and to teach them how to measure for themselves, not only by our actions, but also by using metaphors, similes, language, and concepts that they can understand. When the opportunity arises to "show" our children how much we love them, or alternatively, to let them "see" how little we are truly upset with them, we should drop everything and seize that opportunity. It could be as simple as dropping a quarter on the floor or pointing to the other side of the freeway.

Chapter 3

MANNERS MATTERS

GOOD MANNERS ARE EVERYTHING. Knowing what to do and when to do it makes all the difference in *every* social situation.

A working familiarity with the basic social graces is a foundational key to all the relationships your children will develop in their lifetimes: the friendships with siblings and peers and schoolmates, the studentships with teachers and administrators, the apprenticeships with coaches and mentors. The course of children's social advancement through life is determined in large part by their grace and manners.

The less friction your children cause, the kinder the world will be to them. The less they are noticed for their social inabilities, the more they will be recognized for their unique abilities. The less awkward they are as children, the more graceful and polished they become as adults.

Manners matter.

#26

THE WHISPER GAME

My dear friends Amanda and Bruce have two children: Devon and Isabel. These children are brilliant, passionate, and full of questions and possibilities and then more questions. There is always a buzz of excitement around their house, what with all the inquiries, competitions, explanations, and racing from room to room.

As you might expect, the children are very different from each other.

Isabel walks into every room with a smile on her face, fully expecting to be welcomed and surprised by whatever she finds there. She is quiet and studious and appreciates a good read. Her brother, on the other hand, practically flies into rooms asking what is going on that he does not know about and wondering why he was not included in the first place. She approaches a scene, he bursts upon it. They are two different joys.

But sometimes this is a loud house, and sometimes so loud that one might not hear oneself think clearly or have an idea that lasts long enough to be discussed at any length. An exchange of thoughts or ideas would be compromised by the effort required to keep everyone's attention.

As I was visiting them one evening, I noticed that the children were polite and respectful; they were not rude or ill mannered in any way. But there was a great deal of volume and something (or someone) was causing it.

Both children maneuvered for the attention of one or both parents, and both competed for the right to speak, and both wanted to show their music skills. It is safe to say that they saw each other as the principal competition for anything good that was happening in the house.

But son Devon was a little more competitive, and a little louder, and a little more of everything that made noise. It occurred to me that in the throes of his natural exuberance, he might not know how to operate his volume control button, or even know where it was.

I asked Amanda and Bruce if I could introduce the family to a quieting idea. With their consent I gathered the whole family around me and told them that we were going to try something new, something very, very quiet.

I explained softly that for the next ten minutes we were all going to play the Whisper Game. All anyone had to do to play was whisper. The winners, those who could control themselves and whisper for all ten minutes, would get an extra something before going to bed. I checked my watch, and we began.

Suddenly the house became amazingly quiet. Instantly quiet. Silly quiet, as if it were a different place. There was more room to think. Every idea was precious. It was funny listening to everyone use a different voice.

The phone rang and Amanda answered it in a whispered tone. An idea occurred to Bruce and he whispered it to his children. The dog barked and everyone shushed him. It was all going along just beautifully, and then two things happened that made the evening even more remarkable.

A few minutes into the game, I whispered to Devon, "Did you ever know you could be this quiet? For this long?" He shook his head no. I whispered, "It's so nice when it's quiet . . . isn't it?" He nodded yes. His sister was watching and came over and gave me the biggest hug . . . as though that same idea had been in her head but could not find a way out. As though I had echoed the thought she was thinking, as though something got set free. It made me think that maybe she wanted the house to be a little quieter, too.

The second thing happened later on, when the game was long over and everybody was speaking normally again. Devon came into the kitchen to ask his father a question. But in a different voice, with a different tone and a different volume. Very sweet and very pleasant. He had found his volume control and figured out how to use it.

The Whisper Game only requires a timepiece and a simple reward, but it can change everything about a house in a matter of a few minutes. Play the game and the result is a reset of the volume, a reminder to children that they do not need to shout to be heard.

Want a quieter house? Try the Whisper Game.

27

FIRST BITE / LAST BITE

I took seven-year-old Thomas to Paris several years ago. We were there for a week as part of the Paris Film Festival's celebration of his grandfather, writer/director Preston Sturges.

In anticipation of the trip, I tried to prepare Thomas for what he should expect. I told him that we would be encountering many strange meals and tastes and customs, as this was a completely different culture. I explained that we might be eating such delicacies as escargot (snails), pâté de foie gras (goose liver jam), or coquille Saint Jacques (scallops with vermouth).

He was not enthused.

That is, until I came up with a surefire value-added incentive for him to taste new tastes, a mechanism that rewarded him for showing new-food courage. I called it the First Bite/Last Bite rule.

Under the terms of the rule, Thomas agreed to have one real bite of any food that I put in front of him. This would be the "first bite."

In exchange, he earned the right to finish anything I was eating or drinking, except alcohol, of course. This would be the "last bite." I sold him by pointing out that the many delicious last bites he would enjoy (of cookies, candy bars, sodas, chocolate cake, ice-cream sundaes, milkshakes, etc.) would more than make up for a few unusual-tasting first bites that he would have to endure.

On the second night we were in Paris, Thomas and I took the Metro (the Paris subway) to La Coupole. This is one of the most amazing restaurants in the world. Soccer teams can squeeze in around the huge tables and stuff themselves after big matches alongside couples in the midst of intimate romantic dinners. We fit in as much as anyone else did.

I could not wait to try the famed La Coupole escargot, smothered in rich oils and garlic sauce. When the dish arrived, Thomas looked horrified.

I said, "Thomas . . . First Bite / Last Bite," and held out a dripping mollusk.

He gulped at me in protest, but knowing that he had to eat just one bite gave him all the courage he needed.

He opened his mouth, popped in the delicacy, had a few quick chews, and quickly washed it down. I remember him shaking his head back and forth as if to say, "That was pretty awful," but he played by the rules and was rewarded for doing so. He spent the rest of the trip having earned the right to eat the last bite of everything we ordered, particularly desserts and cookies and other delicious things that the French cuisine had to offer.

This rule has worked out so well that it continues to have a place in our lives, and not just on trips, but every day.

First Bite / Last Bite can help your children avoid developing fussy-eater complex, and gives them plenty of reasons to be courageous and more polite at the dinner table. It also allows them to enjoy new tastes and new experiences that they may not otherwise be willing to try. The pleasure of hundreds of delectable last bites will more than make up for the discomfort of a few unsavory first bites.

Any time you bring your children face-to-face with another culture and its food and customs, there will be much resistance to the different tastes and smells of the food and the water. It is only natural that they will feel some trepidation, much as Thomas did in Paris.

The First Bite / Last Bite rule helps your children overcome their natural resistance to trying new things while it promotes and rewards new-food courage.

28

THREE ESSENTIAL TABLE MANNERS

Teach your children the basic rules of manners and politeness at the dinner table and they will never embarrass themselves when they eat.

Dinner at your house may bear little resemblance to a meal at Abigail Van Buren's, but your children should know what they are supposed to know and how they are supposed to act at the table when sharing a meal with friends and family.

The dinner table is where little boys become little gentlemen, where little girls become little ladies.

Three simple guidelines are the foundation for all good table manners. They are:

1. CHEW WITH THE MOUTH CLOSED. It's no fun sitting next to a child who chews with his or her mouth open. Loud, obnoxious cows like to eat this way but people should not. No exceptions, please!

2. TALK WITH THE MOUTH EMPTY. A companion to the first guideline. Imagine what the other people at the table will have to endure while your child is telling stories around huge mouthfuls of food.

3. HOLD A KNIFE AND FORK LIKE A PAINTER HOLDS A BRUSH. One of the most unappealing things about dining with people who have poor table manners is watching them wield their utensils the way a caveman would wield a stick or a bone. If your child holds his knife and fork in a closed fist, and looks as if he should be dining with the Flintstones, it is no one's fault but yours, dear parent. Teach him to hold his utensils like a painter holds a paintbrush. Delicate and graceful, pointed forward, articulated with grace.

Teach your children to observe these three guidelines and you can eat with them, without embarrassment, almost anywhere you like.

29

REVERSE DINNERS

Sometimes eating can be such a bore. The same routine followed again and again, over and over, meat and vegetables, soup and a sandwich, whatever you say, Mom. Chew, swallow, clean up. Same thing, just a different day.

Vegetables can be especially wearing. Cauliflower, broccoli, okra, lima beans, carrots, brussels sprouts, and so on. Some might wonder: Who thought that these would make good food?

At a certain point your daughter may turn to you and ask, "Why does everything that's good for me taste like it's *not* good for me?" And she has a point. From most children's perspectives, there are very few good-for-you foods that taste good.

After many years of watching my boys lose their enthusiasm for food right in the middle of the meal, I have come to realize that a child's sense of taste can only handle so much wear and tear. It will often give out somewhere in the middle of things, just when the meat is getting cold and the butter is getting too soft. By the time dessert does arrive, it can taste like more of the same, just colder.

Maybe tired taste buds are to blame.

So why not switch things up? Why not give your daughter the food *she* thinks tastes good first, and the food that *is* good last? Switch the order of the menu from front to back. Start with pie à la mode; end with liver and onions. Start with cake; end with steak.

Not for every meal, of course, but occasional Reverse Dinners can break the monotony of too many healthful green vegetables and make eating fun again. Especially on vacations, or snow days, long weekends, when hearts have been broken, or when sad duties are being performed.

Your daughter must agree beforehand that she will eat every single bite of real food that you give her, no matter what, no questions asked. Or else there are no more Reverse Dinners that month. It is practically a contract between the two of you.

Your daughter learns to take responsibility for her own actions—i.e., her eating, and thus herself—and earns the trust you have in her to keep her word and finish all the vegetables and legumes you keep making her eat.

30

OPPOSITE POINTING

When we were all savages living on a savanna somewhere, pointing must have been part of the primitive early warning system. I imagine this skill saving countless of my ancestors from being eaten by countless lions and tigers, and being handed down carefully from one generation of hunter-gatherers to the next, along with fire, the wheel, and halitosis.

So over the millennia, pointing morphed into an instinct and became part of the basic wiring of human beings. And here we are in the present day, where we find that the uniquely human trait of pointing has been entrusted to our children, who love to use it, especially in small quiet rooms where someone is missing a leg or wearing an eye patch.

Children point because it is their instinct to point. From the first moment out of the womb, they are constantly pointing at things they find interesting.

Unfortunately, a mannered society does not approve of pointing and regards it as rude and uncivilized. What a dilemma. What's a parent to do?

Allow your children to follow their instinct and still not be rude. Teach them Opposite Pointing. Teach them to point exactly in the *opposite* direction of where they want you to look. This rule allows them to point out to you everything they see that is unique or interesting or fascinating or different, but not in a way that causes offense to the person being pointed at.

31

SAY THE AWKWARD
WITH A QUESTION

Toilet paper stuck to the bottom of a shoe is hilarious, unless it happens to be your shoe. An undefeated spinach leaf that covers the two front teeth is a big laugh until you see the photo of yourself being used as a screen saver by the office loudmouth. Calling someone by the wrong name in front of a large group of coworkers is a real knee-slapper unless you are the one who saw Malcolm McDowell (the actor from *A Clockwork Orange*) and somehow confused him with Malcolm McLaren (the producer of the Sex Pistols). They look nothing like each other at all.

Yes, all of these were me.

Mark Twain once said that humor is anything funny that happens to someone else. Though this might be true, it is less so when the someone else is a child, particularly your child.

How do you tell your son that he is about to make a fool of himself without making it worse? How do you allow your daughter a little dignity while trying to save her any additional indignity?

For many adults, the first instinct, urge, and quick response is to blurt out what's wrong, and then have a big laugh. But with a child—especially with a child—anything that embarrasses can cause real harm, indeed, irreparable harm, possibly, to the sensitized and always developing sense of self.

You must let him know the truth, especially in an awkward situation, in the gentlest and kindest manner possible.

Accuse him of doing or saying something silly and he will feel attacked. Laugh at his minor misfortunes and he will feel ridiculed. Tell someone else what he did wrong before you tell him and he will feel betrayed, and rightly so.

The kindest way to tell your child something uncomfortable or embarrassing is to put it in the form of a question: a private inquiry instead of a public accusation, a curiosity that is not a condescension. Be inquisitive but not judgmental. Say the awkward with a question.

Quietly ask your son, "If you had a big piece of food stuck between your teeth, would you want me to tell you?" Or privately say to your daughter, "If there was a long streamer of toilet paper attached to the bottom of your shoe, would you want to know about it?" You will have given your son or daughter the chance to correct the mistake before anybody else notices.

He can pull up his zipper or wipe that thing off his nose, or remember to thank Grandma for the slippers before she throws her teeth at him.

Here are some other awkward questions your child will appreciate your asking:

1. If you were pronouncing a word incorrectly, would you want to know about it?
2. If you hurt Mommy's feelings when you called her a rhinoceros, would you want me to tell you?

3. If you were totally wrong about your facts regarding the Yankees–Red Sox rivalry, could I point this out?

4. If your pants were too short and your zipper was down, would you want to know?

Anticipate the embarrassing moment; give your son some warning, and a chance to fix whatever it is before it fixes him.

The hidden beauty of this rule is that you will be providing your son with a model for how to tell *you* something that is difficult or awkward to say. So when he wants to alert you that you have done something foolish, or that you are about to do something graceless, he knows that he can tell you, and he knows *how* he can tell you.

Teach him to say the awkward with a question.

32

THE SIGNIFICANCE OF
A FIRM HANDSHAKE

The Foshay Learning Center is a K–12 public school in inner city Los Angeles. The neighborhoods surrounding the school are economically challenged and gang influenced. Politeness and manners have little value on the streets where these students experience daily life.

I have been working with students from this school for the last several years. They are an amazing group of young men and women, and I consider it a privilege to have been a mentor to many of them.

On my first visit, I realized right away that many of them did not know how to greet someone new in their lives. No one stood up when I introduced myself, no one knew how to properly shake my hand, and not one of them was able to hold my gaze.

I made it my initial priority to teach every single student I met there just exactly how to greet someone new, how to shake hands, and how to look that person right in the eye. Hundreds of them know now to shake my hand and stare me in the eye when they see me in the school hallways.

Not knowing how to properly meet someone new can put a

child at a distinct disadvantage when it comes to any new social situation that he or she will encounter.

Whether it is a new school, a new teacher, a new coach, or a new parent, your son will have only one chance to make his first impression. If he is not sure what exactly to do to start things off, the shadow of that awkwardness might gloom the new relationship.

Learning to shake hands properly can be a balancing antidote to shyness and awkwardness. It can give your son a sense of comfort and familiarity in any gathering and help promote self-respect and grace.

Imagine that you have brought your son to visit a beautiful house, full of candles and light and other children—but you have not taught him how to open the door and walk in. That is what shaking hands is: opening the door between him and the rest of the world. Shaking hands is a way to greet and welcome another person into his life.

The handshake will be a big part of the first impression that your child will make on the world for the rest of his life. Teach him how to do this correctly, and the first impression that he makes will most likely be a positive one.

But hand in hand with a handshake is a strong look in the eye. Your son will gain a much greater understanding of the people in his life if he can look them right in the eye when he shakes their hand. He will give the impression of confidence, and the appearance of being respectful and well mannered, regardless of what he might actually be feeling on the inside.

When a young man looks away during a handshake, as so many did on my first few visits to Foshay, or shuffles his feet, or mumbles a greeting, I cannot help but think that he has some-thing to hide. The chance to make a good first impression is lost forever.

Shaking hands is one of the social conventions that must be mastered at the youngest possible age, along with a good look in the eye. Practice early and often.

#33

THANK-YOU NOTES

In an age of e-mail and text messages, IMs and MySpace, YouTube and Facebook, the classic Thank-You Note has fallen victim to the convenience of instant-gratification communication. Now just more litter left behind on the information superhighway, the Thank-You Note is as vital to human communiqués as the appendix and tonsils are to human life.

But it does not have to be this way. It does not have to end like this.

There are so many good things about the Thank-You Note. It still has plenty to offer and teach our children. It is the best practice ever invented for teaching them to be appreciative, and it is practically incomparable when it comes to showing children how to be respectful.

Yes, the Thank-You Note is old-fashioned, and possibly a little too formal. Maybe it takes a minute. But it is the most gracious gesture possible. It is a sign of complete respect to the person or persons who went to all the trouble of buying your child a gift or otherwise recognizing him.

The basic premise of the Parking Lot Rules is that it is not possible to show too much respect.

Encourage and facilitate the use of the Thank-You Note. Look for reasons. When you buy birthday invitations, buy thank-you cards at the same time. When you are out looking for holiday gifts, buy the thank-yous that will be going out after the holidays. When your daughter is graduating or matriculating, help her write a Thank-You Note to her teacher who got her through the year. When your son has enjoyed a great year of sport, help him write a Thank-You Note to his coach.

The Thank-You Note cannot be replaced. It is the quintessential sign of acknowledgment and appreciation and respect.

34

THE BILL WALTON RULE
If You Can't Be On Time, Be Early

Bill Walton is one of the greatest basketball players ever to bounce a ball on a wood floor. He has been a champion on every level at which he has played, in high school (Helix High in San Diego), college (UCLA), and the pros (Boston and Portland). He was elected to the Basketball Hall of Fame in his first year of eligibility and was named one of the Fifty Greatest NBA Players.

Thanks to his insight and candor, and often brutal honesty, he is also the lead analyst for ESPN/ABC coverage of the NBA.

My Sam and I were watching television and listening to Marv Albert and Mr. Walton cover the first game of the 2004 U.S.A. Olympic basketball team. This team featured such superstars as Allen Iverson, Tim Duncan, Lamar Odom, and LeBron James. Surprisingly, both Iverson and James were watching the crucial first contest sitting on the bench in their street clothes!

Mr. Walton tersely explained that they had been suspended for showing up fifteen minutes late for the first team practice. Walton was completely unforgiving of both men. He particularly railed against Iverson for setting a bad example for the rookie LeBron, and praised coach Larry Brown for instituting the punishment.

Then he said, "To all you kids listening at home, let me tell you something. If you can't be on time, be early."

Have you ever heard someone say something so exactly right that it instantly fits into your life? That's what this line was to me—perfectly, exactly, precisely correct. I had always tried to be on time, but now I had a great little axiom that I could rely on to make sure I was on time. I had never heard it said so well.

I looked over at Sam and said, "So what do you think of that?" He said, "It sounds good to me, Dad." And from that day to this, we are *always* on time—because we are always a little early. This simple guideline as set forth by Bill Walton is now, and will always be, a key element of all of our scheduling.

There is no excuse for being late. There are no benefits, there is no upside, there is no win, nothing is gained. To be late is disrespectful.

If you can't be on time, be early.

35

PLEASE-AND-THANK-YOU RACES

When taking your daughter to eat out at a restaurant, every effort possible must be made to ensure that she is polite and well mannered, respectful to her server, and considerate of all the other diners in the place.

There is nothing quite as disconcerting as an unmannered child at a nearby table who might lick the ketchup bottle, or turn the water glass upside down, or ignore the parents.

One way to inspire your child to be polite and well mannered while eating in restaurants is to give her an incentive to be more polite. Offer her an immediate reward for being gracious.

Please-and-Thank-You Races can be that incentive. The races operate on a very simple mechanism: The child who says "please" and "thank you" the most during the course of the evening wins. She wins two desserts, or the right to ride home "shotgun" or to pick the movie, or a dollar. Whatever it is, it has to be immediate.

Each child keeps his or her own score, with points awarded for every time that he or she says "please" or "thank you," and points taken away for every time he or she should have said so but did not. Each child announces his or her total score at the end of the meal. You deduct points for any fouls committed, arrive at a total for each player, and then announce a winner.

Please-and-Thank-You Races keep every child's eyes on the

same prize—the importance of being polite and well mannered at the restaurant table.

The race is also an interesting diversionary tactic that can contribute to table manners management of children, especially when there are going to be several restaurant meals in a row, such as on vacation, road trips, skiing adventures, at amusement parks, etc.

Making politeness fun and competitive is just one of the intended consequences of Please-and-Thank-You Races.

#36

DESSERT DEMERITS

Dessert Demerits is another table manners management tool, another way to make eating politely one of the first things your child thinks about when eating.

A child is given a demerit for any infraction of good manners at the table: failing to say "please" and "thank you," using the wrong silverware, talking with the mouth open, holding the silverware like a caveman, etc.

If your son gets five demerits, he gets no dessert, or whatever gentle punishment is appropriate to your family or group.

Yes, he can appeal your ruling, as long as he does it politely. And yes, he can erase a demerit by being incredibly polite for the rest of the meal, if you decide so.

Dessert Demerits keeps you in control of the table, and keeps your child thinking about good manners throughout the meal.

37

ANGELS ANGELS EVERYWHERE

When I was a senior in high school, I performed community service as part of my graduation requirement.

Rather than clean pigeon scat off the town's statues or pick up trash on the highway, I chose to be a teaching assistant in the Challenged Student Program at my school. This was the designation for that group of young men and women who were not quite ready for school, either emotionally or otherwise. Some had autism or other learning disabilities, one could hardly see, and one was born with a physical issue and had to get around in a wheelchair.

Though it only lasted through a part of my senior year, this was an experience that shaped my consciousness and changed forever the way I saw the world, especially those in it who may not enjoy all the advantages I enjoy.

As I watched the challenged students go about their daily lives, I came to realize that children with disabilities were ostracized, whether by cruel intention or by the innocence of human nature acting on its own instinct to reject anything outside of "normal" parameters. This appeared to happen irrespective of the degree of difference, apparently simply because there was any difference at all.

But I also came to realize how incredibly optimistic the challenged students remained in spite of this. The captain of the football team somehow always bumped into Jeremy when he was drinking at the water fountain, one time knocking loose one of Jeremy's front teeth. But every day Jeremy believed the captain of the football team was going to stop.

All of the challenged students were like this. They went to lunch in the cafeteria—at their own special table—with incredible optimism and positivity, expecting that everything would go well, or at least better than yesterday. Usually they were right, but not always. More than once I returned a wadded-up hamburger to the individual who threw it across the room at my group.

When you and your children are out in the real world, you will spot many challenged individuals. They might have multiple sclerosis, Down syndrome, Lou Gehrig's disease, or autism, be blind or deaf, or be an accident victim who is now and forever a paraplegic or quadriplegic. They might be recovering from cancer and have survived chemo, left without a hair on their heads.

But have you ever noticed . . . they rarely, if ever, appear upset or downbeat about their situations. Somehow they have become accustomed to their fate, to their lot in life, to their place in the grand design. They are often optimistic and hopeful, with simple joys. Just getting through another day is often a cause for some kind of celebration.

An angel is someone who knows only how to love. An angel is someone who retains his or her innocence and optimism regardless of the circumstances. Angels hope you will be nice, too. As I came to know the members of the Challenged Student Program, they came to remind me of what angels *must* be like.

I have used the possibility of angels being everywhere and anywhere to teach my children—and all the children in my life—to be patient and understanding with those who are different from them, particularly people who are enduring difficult circumstances.

It is the zenith of rudeness to point out that someone has challenges. It is the height of politeness and good manners to accept someone and his or her challenges. Teach your children to welcome everyone they meet in life, particularly those who are even a little bit different, with patience, tolerance, kindness, respect, and love.

Teach them to look out for all the angels that they might otherwise not have noticed.

Teach them that there are angels angels everywhere.

Chapter 4
NO LOST CHILDREN

THERE IS NOTHING WORSE—absolutely nothing worse—than losing your child. It might only be a few seconds, or a few minutes, but words like *terrified* and *panic-stricken* will hold new meaning from that moment forward. Unfortunately, it happens.

In Las Vegas one weekend, ten minutes after we checked in to the Mirage hotel, three-year-old Thomas saw an open elevator door and walked right in. There were two other adults on that trip besides me and his mother, but for that second only, nobody was watching Thomas. We all looked up at the same time, just as the elevator door closed behind him.

The next few minutes went by as if in a dream. A really bad dream. A dentist-drilling-without-novocaine dream. What kind of parent loses a child, after all? Then, when we were all running out of worst-case scenarios, the elevator door opened. Out walked Thomas, untouched and unfazed. He might not even have known he was lost.

The more crowded the places you take your child, the more precautions you need to take to limit the risks of losing him or her. Here are some ideas, suggestions, and precautions that will reduce the chances of ever losing anyone.

#38

THE JOHN ELWAY RULE

Any time you take your child where there are big crowds, take big precautions along as well. Give yourself the best chance of not losing sight of your child no matter how big the crowd around you gets.

Build a strong, easy-to-spot visual bridge between your son and you so that he is always within your frame of vision.

This is the John Elway Rule: Whenever you are going to be in a crowd, make sure that your child is easy to spot from a near or great distance by dressing him in the jersey of your favorite NFL player.

An NFL jersey is meant to be seen from the top row of an enormous stadium in the middle of a rainstorm. This same jersey can serve as the only visual cue you will need to keep your son in sight while he is busy wandering away from you somewhere in Stapleton Airport.

This simple precaution will add to the acuity of your visual cues, and the quality of your knowledge of his whereabouts at all times. It is very difficult *not* to notice the bright and distinctive brands of an NFL jersey, even hundreds of feet away.

If he does begin to stray off, your eyes will tell you right away. You will sweep the crowd and easily spot John Elway's Denver

Broncos number 7 (bright orange number on a deep blue background) walking somewhere he should not be walking.

Good use of this rule will ensure that your child is easier to spot and harder to lose than if he were in normal everyday child clothes.

If he is ever seriously lost, and you need to contact security, the first question they will ask is, "What is he wearing?" It will be simpler and quicker to describe him as a three-feet-tall version of John Elway than "a cute little boy with brown hair and a beige T-shirt" or "I think he might have been wearing shorts and a tank top." At that moment, valuable seconds might be lost forever.

Let the John Elway Rule guide you, and never lose sight of your child.

39

STAY WHERE YOU ARE AND FLY LIKE AN ANGEL

I took a group of children to the Long Beach Aquarium in California several years ago, including my nephew Elio. At one point he took a right when the rest of us took a left. The panic that ensued choked him—he told me that he literally could not breathe. He was "lost" for less than a minute but was crying and nearly hyperventilating when we found him. This was many years ago and I still do not think that he has forgiven me.

We teach our children to look both ways before they cross the street. We teach them not to talk to strangers or get into strange cars. We teach them so many other important cautions. We should also teach them how to be lost.

By knowing what to do *if* they get lost, they will be more aware of the fact that they *can* get lost. This awareness will help reduce the chances of the sad event ever taking place.

As a result of the experience with Elio at the aquarium, it occurred to me that it would be a great idea to teach the children in my life what to do if any of them ever did get lost. They would then know instinctively how to react and how to get found as quickly as possible.

The rule that I came up with is Stay Where You Are and Fly Like an Angel. It is simple and easy for a lost child to remember. It has two parts.

First, the moment your child realizes that she has become separated from you or the group, the first thing that she must do is stay right where she is—*right where she is*. She should not run off looking for security, or the lost and found, or someone who looks like a parent. She should recognize that she is lost and stop right there.

Second, she needs to call as much attention to herself as possible. There is no reason for her to be embarrassed that she has gotten lost. After she knows to stop right where she is, teach her next to wave her arms up and down, as broadly and slowly as possible, to Fly Like an Angel.

If passersby ask her what she is doing waving her arms like that, she can just say that she is waiting for her mommy or daddy to come back.

The parental instinct is a very strong and effective mechanism that constantly updates and tells you where your child is, almost like sonar on a submarine. If you can stay attuned to its warnings, it will let you know that you have not seen your child for too long, and to start looking for her. More than likely you will realize that she is lost just about the same time she realizes that she is lost.

Reverse your steps and walk back the way you came.

All you need to do is look for your very terrified daughter, hopefully following the John Elway Rule and wearing a brightly colored NFL jersey, waving her arms up and down like a little angel . . .

. . . trying to fly back to you.

. . .

Teach your daughter to follow the two simple steps outlined in this rule and if she ever does get lost, your chances of reuniting with her quickly are that much greater.

When you do reunite with her, ten seconds or ten minutes later, somehow avoid the urge to scold or punish her for having gotten herself lost. Rejoice that you found her, safe and unharmed.

However awful it was for you to lose her, you can only imagine what it was like for her to be lost, panicked and terrified and guilty all at the same time.

Teach her to stay where she is and fly like an angel.

40

WALK BIG AND TALL

We parents should dress as distinctively as possible when we are taking our children to crowded places. Many children means many, many distractions. The more visual cues and incentives we give our children to keep their eyes on us, the greater the likelihood that they will.

Consider the use of this rule a legitimate reason to wear those loud and outrageous fashion-backward golf shirts and bright, flowing polka-dot summer dresses that would never get out of the closet otherwise.

Also available is a variation on the John Elway Rule. We can proudly wear the jersey of our favorite NFL player, and then repeatedly remind our children why we are dressed like that.

Even if this takes us to the point of silliness, it is all for a good cause if it will help our children know where we are at all times, particularly in crowded places.

#41

MATCHING WRISTBANDS

In any large traveling group, brightly colored wristbands can easily serve to identify all of the members. If a little one is distracted or otherwise just walking away from the flock, his or her wristband will serve as a further visual cue to all of the adults that something is about to be amiss.

These bands come in Day-Glo orange and green and red and the cost is pretty minimal considering that the visual reminder of where your children are and where they might be going is priceless. Remember to write your phone number on every wristband—making the return as simple as possible if your son or daughter does wander off.

Wear them on wrists *and* ankles for an extra layer of visual security.

#42

DOG TAGS

My son Thomas went to New York with his uncle and cousins a few years ago, and it was his first trip away from home without a parent. His mother and I were understandably very concerned about his safety and welfare—perhaps *too* concerned about his safety and welfare.

Against the advice of everyone in the family, and the howling of my son that it would be embarrassing to him, we decided that he could only go if he wore a laminated information card on a lanyard. In essence, dog tags.

On this card were his name, birthday, several phone numbers (including mine, his mother's, his nanny's and his uncle's, and those of others on the trip), the address of the hotel he was staying in, airline and flight numbers, and, just for good measure, his shoe size and blood type, and his favorite candy bar.

He hated it, but that was only because he never needed it.

By wearing dog tags, he was completely conscious of his whereabouts the whole trip. Had he become lost or separated from the group, and none of the other rules saved him, he was well armed to find his way back to the hotel or to get help reaching out to any of us whose names and numbers appeared on his dog tags.

He wore his dog tags under his outer shirt or in his pants

pocket. We did not want to make him vulnerable to predators by giving them the head start of knowing his name or any other key information.

Dog tags are a great idea for a trip that lasts several days or many miles to a foreign city or other unknown locale, where your child may have his guard down. Dog tags make him continually aware of the possibility that he *could* get lost, and gives him a tool to get found just as quickly as possible.

#43

THE CABOOSE RULE

When a family or group travels together, you will often see a very young member who thinks that he or she is "leading the way." This child motors along just ahead of the main group, like a pilot fish swimming ahead of a whale pod. It is rarely the case that this child will wander off and get lost. Everyone else in the family is behind, watching.

But children who get lost often do so because they are *not* able to keep up with the family or group on the long walks and forced marches that inevitably take place at events like fairs or theme parks, or when the family is hiking or skiing.

These younger and usually slower children might get a little tired, and then start to lag behind. Then they become distracted by something, and next thing you know, when they look up, they cannot recognize anyone who is near them. They are lost.

The Caboose Rule assigns to a designated adult or an older child the critical responsibility of being the very last one in the group, the last car of the train, the last safety net available. The purpose of the Caboose Rule is to ensure that there is one last line of defense. The buck stops here!

The "caboose" is particularly responsible for the littler and more vulnerable members of the group or family who might too easily wander off.

A shepherd does not lead a flock—he follows it. He can keep a better eye on his animals and any harm that might befall them by watching from behind. He can anticipate when one of them is losing its way and step in to rescue.

While this is roughly the same idea, I call it the Caboose Rule because that just sounds a lot better than the "Sheep Rules."

44

ANONYMOUS CLOTHING/
ANONYMOUS CARS

Many children play sports, and it is often an option when buying uniforms to have the children's names sewn or embroidered onto jerseys or jackets.

Children love the individuality of their names on their clothes, since it makes them look more like their sports heroes, but the upside does not balance against the downside—the risks being taken, the vulnerability of the circumstance.

Put a child's name on his clothing and you have given any dangerous character an advantage. *They know the child's name!* Too easily they can cross the first line of defense: familiarity.

If your child becomes lost or separated from the group or from the family at a crowded mall or an event, chances are that he will be terrified and guilty and not thinking straight at all. Many of the usual danger filters will be shutting down. The friendly man who reaches for him will probably seem like a nice person simply because he knows your child's name.

The world is dangerous enough as it is. Let your children be anonymous when they are out in it.

This same concept and rule applies to those families who proudly display the names of their family members on the back window of their SUVs: You place the youngest members of your family in the greatest danger. Why tell a complete stranger what the children's names are? There is no good reason, there is no point, and there is no win.

Anonymous Clothing/Anonymous Cars. Safely incognito is better than the vulnerable alternative.

45

YOUR CHILD HAS TO KNOW
WHERE YOU ARE

One of the most awkward and embarrassing things to see in a store or a mall is a parent chasing after a child. It's a little like watching a dog walk around on its hind legs: momentarily interesting but clearly just wrong.

The child thinks it is some kind of game, like tag, or hide-and-seek. She may be too young to know the danger she is putting herself in as she runs across a mall or hides behind the display of oversize vegetables at the local market. It is all great fun until something happens that might easily have been avoided.

A solution is to reverse the responsibility. Any time you are out of the house, make it your daughter's one and only job to know where you are at all times. She has to keep her eyes on you, not the other way around. She can be free and mobile, and out of the basket or shopping cart, or not holding your hand, just so long as she knows where you are *at all times*.

Training is not difficult. Your child loves her freedom and she will do what needs to be done to keep it. In the beginning, as you teach the basic workings of this rule, she may well forget to keep up with you. Without anger or rancor, explain how the rule was broken. Return her gently to the shopping cart seat or wherever she was being corralled, and soon enough she will learn.

The earlier you can start on this rule, the better, and right as she learns to walk will be soon enough. This rule will also encourage your daughter to know where *she* is at all times, and to know where she needs to be. It will likewise raise her level of self-awareness and acuity to danger.

The principles that are taught by this rule may have a positive residual effect. As your child gets a little older and gets taken to baseball games and airports, her level of vulnerability increases, and her need to be self-aware increases as well.

She learns—to the point where it becomes a part of her instinct—that she always has to know where you are.

46

KEEP 'EM WIRED

Make it easy for your child to stay in touch when the family is at a fair, an amusement park, a sporting event, or a ski resort.

Cellphones or walkie-talkies give children incredible freedom. If your child does not have his own phone already, equip him with one borrowed from one of the adults or older children on the trip.

Before you hand it over, program that cellphone so that it can easily speed-dial or "one-button call" your phone in the event of any problems or requests.

For children too young to carry a phone, teach them to carry a tune—one that will help remind what mom's or dad's cellphone number is.

My own number fits perfectly with Twinkle, Twinkle, Little Star," while Antonina's matches Tommy Tutone's "867-5309."

Whether they use their own phone or borrow someone else's, they will know how to reach you, if you keep 'em wired.

#47

BUDDY DIVING

When someone is qualifying for scuba diving certification, one of the key guidelines that is drilled into the diver's head is the life-saving necessity of always diving with another diver.

"Never dive alone" is the number one rule of scuba. They call it Buddy Diving.

Buddy Diving reduces the chances of a diver ending up in a dangerous situation that he or she might not be equipped to handle alone. Divers are instructed to stay within an arm's length of their buddy.

Safety is everything when one is diving, especially in deep water. There is no room for error and hardly any time left over to correct any mistakes. If a diver gets distracted, or caught up in some debris, or encounters some sort of equipment malfunction, he or she could easily be lost or left behind, and there is nothing worse than being left behind on a scuba dive.

Similarly, safety is everything when you and your children are anywhere where there are big crowds and big distractions. Just as in diving, there is little room for error and very little time to correct foolish mistakes.

A parent who is taking a large group of children on an adventure somewhere can learn from scuba divers. One way to keep children from getting lost is to assign each child to a buddy, and it is usually best if the buddy is someone about his or her same age and same size. They can help to look after each other.

A buddy always has to know where his buddy is, what his buddy is doing, and why, and stays no more than an arm's length away.

Chapter 5
DISCIPLINES AND PUNISHMENTS

DISCIPLINES AND PUNISHMENTS are the least enjoyable and most stressful aspects of the parenting experience. To punish your children is the exact opposite of why you brought them into the world. Deciding and administering the fair punishment will tax your reserves of goodwill and cheat you out of the love that you deserve to get from your beautiful children.

Here are some ideas to consider when the unfortunate day arrives when you must consider the discipline and punishment of your little ones.

48

THE TRUTH REDUCES THE PUNISHMENT BY 90 PERCENT

From the time we are born, we are told that honesty is the best policy. From George Washington and the cherry tree to Bill Clinton and the interns, somehow it always comes down to telling the truth.

But to a child, the value and importance of the truth are not always as obvious as they should be. When faced with the prospect of dealing with an angry parent or telling a little white lie, a child will often choose the little white lie. To him, it's a quick way out. Whatever the problem, it goes away, at least for a while.

Parents should be aware of this tendency to cover a truth with a fib, and prevent it from becoming a habit that finds traction in a child's life.

There needs to be a clear benefit to telling the truth, an incentive that cannot be denied, a logic that makes sense to a child of any age: a six-year-old who just flushed her turtle down the toilet, or her older brother who has good reason for hiding a shabby report card.

Draw a connection between a lie and its consequences by linking the truth and the punishment. Make the telling of the truth the only option that your son or daughter will seriously consider.

Make it a rule of your parenting that the truth will reduce the punishment by 90 percent.

When your son tells the truth, reward him immediately. Tell him what the punishment would have been had he kept the truth from you, and then give him a much-reduced punishment as his reward.

Once he understands that the risk-reward mechanism works completely to his advantage, he will look forward to telling the truth and accepting responsibility for his actions. The telling of the truth will become a Get Out of Jail Free card, and you want him to use it that way, as often as necessary.

A few years ago, I came home to find my then third-grade son Thomas near tears as he anticipated my arrival. I was not three steps in the door when he rushed over to me. Breathless and tearful, he stood there looking up at me.

I asked him, "Thomas-Tom. What's the matter?"

He managed to stammer out, "Does the t-truth still refuse the p-punishment by nighty percets?" He didn't get all the words right, but he had the right idea. I told him that it always did and always would. Then I said, "Is there something that you want to tell me about? Is there something that happened?"

He tried to be very brave, but his will failed and his beautiful little face crumpled from the edges in, and a flood of tears soon followed.

Out poured the story of his accidentally hitting another boy and being reprimanded by his teacher. He finished triumphantly, ". . . and that's the truth, Dad." He was very serious and his eyes never left mine.

I was very proud of him and I told him so. I complimented him on his courage and I praised him for his honesty. I told him that I was proud of the way that he had handled himself. I told him that *if* his teacher had called to tell me all these sad details, the punishment would have been two weeks without TV or video games, and no sleepovers, either. His eyes widened as he realized how seriously I viewed the infraction.

But since he had told me the truth, I told him that the punishment was reduced by 90 percent, from two weeks to two nights and that this evening was the first night. A huge smile broke out over his face. He clenched his fist as a symbol of complete victory. "Excellent," he said, hugged me, and walked away on a cloud of praise and self-satisfaction.

Thomas told the truth and it set him free. His reward was immediate and tangible, and something valuable to him. By telling the truth, he had already accepted responsibility for his actions, and thus the need for punishment was significantly reduced—it was almost unimportant. The link between truth and reward was forged in him forever.

Thomas has remained an incredibly honest child who can always be counted on to tell the truth, no matter how difficult the circumstances. Inspire this same metric in your child by letting the truth reduce the punishment by 90 percent.

49

THE TEN-SECOND RULE

It is so often the case that punishments are decided when parents are the least prepared to make such important determinations.

It might be just after an errant baseball whistles through a living room window, for instance, or upon the arrival of the report card that reveals a lowly D in Basic English, or as you hang up on an irate neighbor who called to report that your little angel was just spotted dressing a historically significant pine tree in toilet paper.

This is probably not the ideal moment to decide a fair and just punishment.

Save yourself from handing down something that is harsh and unforgiving. Save your children and the rest of your family from having to live with a decision that you might regret the moment after you make it. A moment of anger might only last an instant, but it can leave a mark that lasts a lifetime.

Before you do anything, take a couple of deep breaths. Consider the significance of all that you are about to do, *before* you do it. One alligator . . . two alligator . . . three alligator. Take just ten seconds before you make your first move.

Then, start asking questions—lots of them. Who, what, where, when, and why, just to get the ball rolling. Ask good follow-up questions and press for additional details. Remind your offspring that the truth reduces the punishment by 90 percent! Very soon *all* the truth will be revealed, and things will become clear that previously were murky.

Punish in your haste and you will regret it at your leisure. Instead, take ten seconds and ask a lot of questions. It will make a great deal of difference in the quality of your determination and the justness and fairness of your disciplines and punishments.

50

THE LIST OF JOYS AND
THE THREAT OF DISCIPLINE

Oldest son Thomas was in sixth grade, struggling to maintain a C-minus average.

He was provided with a tutor and study-skills classes, was enrolled for academic and organizational support, was provided with plenty of incentives—and none of it made the slightest difference. Quite simply, that year Thomas was a poor student who gave a halfhearted effort.

There was no changing this through traditional means, despite all the well-intentioned measures. So when he came home from school one day, he discovered a list posted on his bedroom wall. It represented many of the joys in his life. It was several things that he loved to do, that he would miss most.

He was told that one by one, every single one of these joys would be taken away from him in a progressive enforcement of punishment if he did not improve his grades. Every day that he walked into his room, he saw the list:

1. television
2. video games and Internet access
3. sleepovers, both home and away

4. sports
5. friends

Over the course of the next few months, Thomas lost the right to watch TV. And play video games. And have access to the Internet. And sleepovers.

As each joy was taken away, a red line was drawn through it. It would have broken my heart to take away basketball and soccer, and access to his friends, but if necessary, that would have happened, too.

This was no sudden anger, no rush to judgment, just an immovable resolve to help him get back on track. There was the threat, and then the delivery of a patient and unbending discipline. As it was enforced, step by step, it gave him time to realize that he was completely responsible for what was happening. He learned that he was in control of his life and that his privileges were subject to his living up to his responsibilities.

By the end of the school year, Thomas had finally turned things around. He began to get his homework completed on time and improved all of his grades. One by one, his privileges were restored. The list of joys and the threat of discipline put Thomas in control of his life by making him responsible for his own happiness.

This tool will serve as a steady, oppressive, and factual reminder to your son of what he will lose, what hangs in the balance, what is worth fighting for, and why he needs to get on the program that you have laid out for him.

The list of joys and the threat of discipline can provide inspiration and motivation for your son to do exactly what you need him to do.

FOOD AND PUNISHMENT

Food and punishment have nothing to do with each other. Never deny your child food as part of any punishment. Nor should you ever forbid your daughter a place at the table with her family just because a punishment is being administered.

Eating with the family will give your child a brief reprieve from the punishment, and will give you the chance to be kind and loving while maintaining a state of punishment.

NO REASON TO HIT—EVER

The Parking Lot Rules are very clear on this point. There can be no hitting, ever.

No matter what, why, when, or how, never hit your child. Never touch your son in anger. Never squeeze his arm too tightly or grab him suddenly. Never pull his hair or jerk him out of his seat. Find some other way to get your message through.

Hitting, or in any way causing physical pain or harm to a child, is the antithesis of the Parking Lot Rules. If you want to reach your child, and change his behavior, this must be done without discouraging, diminishing, denigrating, or demeaning. No hitting. Ever.

Violence inspires only more violence.

#53

NO-YELLING RULES

The Parking Lot Rules are very clear on this point, too: no yelling at children. No matter what, why, when, or how, never yell at children.

All of the studies that I could find indicated that yelling might actually damage children's ability to understand and communicate later in life.

They quickly become accustomed to anger and the presence of adrenaline in their system, and this leads them to opt for a quickly triggered and angry response to any conflict, regardless of how minor.

Children who get yelled at soon begin to lose the ability to detect nuance and subtlety in their relationships going forward. Yelling only inspires more yelling.

Children give back what we give them. They want patience, understanding, kindness, the right to be forgiven, the chance to try again, everything that we want. They are mirrors that reflect the lives we provide for them.

Children who are loved will love. Children who are respected will respect. What do you suppose happens to the children who are yelled at by parents who are supposed to love and respect them?

#54

THE POWER OF FORGIVENESS

Your beautiful daughter made a mistake.

She forgot to do her homework, again. She left the TV on all night, again. She did not brush and floss her teeth as you asked, or she was rude to the grandparents or mean to the dog. She forgot to close the freezer door tight and melted all the ice cream, for the sixth time. She played video games past her bedtime and fibbed about it when you caught her in the act.

You had no other option but to punish her. And so you did. Maybe you were a little upset and raised your voice and scared her a little, too.

Right now your daughter is sniffling on the sofa in the guest room, or sitting alone in the middle of the bathroom. She knows that she has disappointed you. She might even think that there is a possibility that you might not love her as much as before. She thinks you do not care how she feels because you walked out of the room while she was crying. She never heard you use that voice before. She is sadder than she has ever been.

Now what?

How do you end it? How do you get to the other side of the punishment? How do you get back to being the loving and supportive parent that you would rather be to this beautiful child? How do you get past all that just happened?

If your daughter got the message, and she is genuinely remorseful, and regretful, and upset with herself, and can truly understand what has happened, then the punishment was a success. She is exactly where you want her to be. Both sides can now move forward.

At the first reasonable opportunity, forgive her completely, and without reservation. Let her back into your good graces, let her back into your heart. Let her begin to rebuild and try to start over. The power of your forgiveness will be the sound of your loving voice, your inquiry about how she is feeling. Your kind touch and gentle voice will be like cool water on her dry throat. A warm and patient hug will begin to prove that all is right with the world again.

Ask her if she understands what happened, and if she knows why you were so upset with her. Gently revisit the details if you must, but really gently, and only if you must.

As the parent, and the discipliner, you are the only one who can make everything right again. The power of forgiveness can make everything right again.

To make a foolish mistake is what children do. To forgive that mistake is what great parents do. As soon as possible.

Your daughter will make mistakes and break the rules. Unfortunately, that is one way she learns. When you find compassion and enough good reasons to forgive her for those mistakes, she then learns what a great parent you are.

Suppose that it was a first offense, or she did not fully understand the rules that were broken. Suppose that your spouse offers additional evidence, or a sibling informs you that things are actually not as bad as they looked at first.

Or suppose that you decide to reconsider the basic facts of the matter, having found some fault with your earlier logic.

You have the right to review your decisions about discipline and punishment at any time, and you should. When you have cooled down a little, you might realize that you were a bit harsh in the heat of the moment. You can cut short the sentence that you just meted out, or even throw it out completely.

Imagine what your child will feel like if you walk back into that room wherever she is and forgive her completely. She will practically burst with relief and happiness, and love you all the more. And this is the whole point.

Let the power of forgiveness guide your parenting during the administering of disciplines and punishments. Your compassion will then be in full bloom, and one of the things that your daughter will learn from her mistake is how much you love her.

WHATEVER YOU DO, AVOID TAUTOLOGY

The word *tautology* describes the speaking habits of someone who repeats himself, whether telling a story or a joke, or sharing some wisdom. He will tell the same tale again and again, but with just a couple of details different.

When speaking to your children about their mistakes and misdeeds, be sure that you do not practice tautology. Simplify your message. Make it easy to understand and easy to remember. Be perfectly clear when you tell your children what they did wrong and why you are upset with them.

At the risk of being redundant and repetitive, and redundant, let me say that tautology is the last thing children need from their parents, especially when they are in trouble.

Whatever you have to say, whatever you do, avoid tautology. Try to say it only once!

FIVE VERY EFFECTIVE
NONVIOLENT PUNISHMENTS

If you must punish your child—and this should be the very last option taken—let it be done with dignity and respect. There is no reason ever to yell or hit, shake, squeeze an arm too tightly, or in any other way physically intimidate your child. Try not to diminish your child as you punish him or her. Instead, be swift and just, respectful, polite, quiet, kind, and always completely nonviolent. Here are five possible punishments that fit these guidelines:

1. THE SILENT TREATMENT. If your child has said something rude or inappropriate, the silent treatment is a punishment of a like kind. A child should be forbidden to talk or communicate in any way, for some amount of time that you feel is fair and just. Perhaps five or ten or fifteen minutes or an hour, depending on the age of the child and the severity of the transgression. If the child speaks at any time during the punishment, start the time over.

2. DO NOT GO TO YOUR ROOM. More than likely, your daughter's room is well fitted with interesting books and games, possi-

bly a TV or her computer or maybe a video game. It is her kingdom and her haven and her sanctuary. Let it be that. Also let it be the *last* place that she is sent for a punishment. Depending upon the severity of the infraction, make her room off-limits for an amount of time roughly commensurate with it. For instance, the child was late for school by ten minutes? An hour without a room is a just punishment.

3. THE WRITING PUNISHMENT. Consolidate the message that you want your child to understand into a brief sentence. Then have him write that sentence over and over and over. If he is young and the mistake was small, ten lines will be all that is needed for "I will do all of my homework." But if he is older, and the mistake was more serious, then punishment should be more serious, such as writing "I will be more responsible with my siblings" two hundred times. Let him know that if even one line is illegible, the entire page may need to be redone. Ever-improving penmanship is only one of several side benefits of this still respectful nonviolent punishment.

4. MAKE HIM APOLOGIZE TO THE WHOLE FAMILY. Gather the family together. The child being punished must stand up in front of the entire family and apologize to everyone for whatever he did that got him in trouble, to the parents as well as the other children. Do not use this technique at a holiday gathering since the punishment may be worse than the offense.

5. HAVE YOUR CHILD RUN LAPS. Somewhere near your house there is a park or field or track or playground. For her punish-

ment, have your daughter do laps around it. Make the number of laps equate to the severity of the mistake that she made. She will endure some physical pain, but it will not be at your hand. She will be sore after, but not bruised or hurting. She will remember the laps and, in the future, may try to avoid the behavior that caused them. If you want to be the punisher and somehow also try to be a concerned and considerate parent, do the laps alongside her.

Chapter 6
PAIN HAPPENS, NOW WHAT?

WHEN CHILDREN ARE PLAYING, no matter how many protections and precautions are in effect, it is practically predictable that someone will get hurt.

Children play hard, and they pay for it with real bumps and bruises, cuts and scrapes, skinned knees and red elbows, and the occasional bloody nose or sprained ankle.

These kinds of minor injuries are impossible to eliminate or even control.

But what happens right after children get hurt *is* controllable. It is up to us to minimize the pain, dry the tears, find a laugh somewhere, reduce the impact of the injury, and get our children back up on their feet and back into the game or the playtime before they lose their will altogether.

What follows are things to do when it all ends in tears.

57

TAKE THE PAIN AWAY

I was at a birthday party with my son Thomas. He was five. The usual assortment of party clowns and watchful parents were gathered for the ritual of the piñata. If you do not know this scam, you are not missing much. A piñata is a replica of an innocent little animal, such as a lamb or baby deer, that is filled with suspect candy and dangled in front of a blindfolded child. The child swings a stick and basically tries to murder the innocent little animal. If the piñata gets hit enough times, it breaks open and spills candy all over the place.

On this day, up came a little boy who thought of himself as quite a slugger. He tapped the ground in front of him like Casey at the Bat, peeked under his blindfold to get his bearings, and then proceeded to swing the stick wildly back and forth like a maniac. Until he hit something. Unfortunately, that something was *not* the piñata. It was the birthday boy! The little boy, Cole, burst into tears and grabbed the arm where he had been struck.

The father must have been embarrassed that his son was crying so hard. Instead of holding him, loving him, and consoling him, the dad was impatient and kept telling his son, "You're fine . . . you're fine . . . just stop crying. That's enough now." But the child was anything but fine and let his dad know it with his tears.

When I saw all this unfolding, I felt bad for Cole and his dad. Then I had an idea: Why not have all of the children at the party share the pain somehow? Instead of isolating Cole, why not make his pain part of the group experience? I asked the group if they wanted to help me take the pain away from Cole. I explained that we would all have to take just a little bit of it ourselves. Everyone wanted some pain.

So I brought all of the children together in a big circle around Cole, and everyone placed their hand on his arm where the injury occurred. Then, on the count of three, I shook the pile of hands (for effect only), and seemingly withdrew the pain from Cole, and sent a little bit of it to everyone who was touching him. It was like magic.

Following my cue, every child grabbed his or her arm, *in the same place as Cole's injury,* and started howling in pain, with drama, gravitas, and hubris all rolled into one. Shouts were heard, like "Wow, that hurts!" and "Oh, my arm, my arm!" and "Ouchie, ouchie!"

It was so much fun taking the pain away from Cole that we had to do it a few more times, just to get all of the pain out of him, by which time Cole was laughing again, too, and he was soon right back in the middle of things enjoying his birthday party.

By taking a few minutes to take the pain away, we gave Cole a chance to be respected for his pain, to recover from his injury, to be the absolute center of attention for a little while, and to have everyone at the party care very much that he felt better.

A minor injury? Take the pain away.

#58

SLOW-MOTION REPLAYS

Have you bumped your head recently? Or walked into a low-hanging chandelier? Ever turned in to a doorway before the door was open all the way? Any time you hit your head, it hurts like crazy, but not only does it hurt, it is embarrassing and one cannot help but feel foolish. That's how a child feels.

Many times when a child is crying and hurt from a minor injury, part of the problem is that he is embarrassed. Yes, his head or his knee hurts a little, but what really hurts is his ego. He has injured his own pride somehow and there is still the scent of injustice in the air.

So once you have determined that the injuries are not life-threatening, and that the child will survive completely, you need to let him know that it was not his fault in any way. And you need to get him laughing again.

One way to accomplish both tasks with the same action is to explain to him precisely and exactly what happened to him—in the most ridiculous and exaggerated detail—and then demonstrate it all in slow motion!

Show him exactly what he looked like while tripping and bumbling and stumbling. The more exaggerated the explanation, the funnier it will be and the sooner his tears will stop. He will see that it was not his fault and that he has nothing to be embarrassed about, either.

It might sound like this:

DAD *(breathless)*: "Welcome to WPPX News. This just in. Sam Sturges was just smacked in the head by a tree in the front yard of his home. For a more detailed report, we switch to the scene."

(Dad now becomes another reporter, his thumb an imaginary microphone.)

"Thank you, Bob. Here is what we know so far. There was Sam, walking down the street, minding his own business, when out of nowhere, and I mean nowhere, out jumped a low-hanging tree branch.

"According to eyewitness reports, the tree smacked Sam right in the forehead! Sam was looking around, wondering who smacked him, when he stumbled over the same tree's roots and fell into the trash can.

"Now let's look at the footage."

(Dad now reenacts the whole thing in slow motion. Sound effects, a slow-motion voice, exaggerated facial expressions, falling over and rolling around, basically whatever it takes to get his Sam smiling again.)

"Now back to you, Bob."

"Thank you for that astonishing report. This has been WPPX News. Around your house, around your town. Good day."

If your child is not laughing with you, start all over and tell him all over again, as many times as you need to. If nothing else, he will love the fact that you are trying so hard to bring back his laughter.

Use Slow-Motion Replays and help your child laugh away his tears.

#59

FREEZE IT / THEN CLEAN IT

At the tail end of a night walk a few years ago, I challenged my two sons and Elio and Anthony, their cousins, to compete against one another in an impromptu two-man downhill bobsled skateboard slalom competition.

This was to take place on a sidewalk near our house, and it turned out to be another bad idea. It was fun at the beginning, with the boys laughing and falling off the boards, but this was before they figured out how to get momentum going down the hill.

Once they figured out the balance and just how to do it, disaster waited patiently for them. Thomas and Elio were halfway down the track on the final run when their skateboards spun out and Elio protected himself by riding Thomas like Seabiscuit until they finally came to a grinding halt next to a cactus!

Despite helmets and wristguards, and my entreaties for everyone to be careful, of course the inevitable happened—someone got hurt and the game was over abruptly. Thomas was howling in tears and pain, with a rude and ugly scrape traveling six inches down his forearm.

Gravel had ground into Thomas's skin and he felt every single grain of it. Since it was all my fault, he was angry at me, too.

Though it was not serious enough to go to the hospital for, it was hurting him like H-E-double-hockey-sticks and I just wanted the pain to stop. I did not want to cause him any more pain cleaning out the cut, either.

Knowing that ice can reduce the swelling and the sensation of pain, I began to apply ice to the skin *all around* the scrape. I never touched the scrape; I just got close to the edges of it. The ice was wrapped in a wet paper towel, and I moved it back and forth like a circular windshield wiper.

In minutes, the scrape and the skin around it were completely numb. I talked to him about football and girls—anything to distract him—and poured hydrogen peroxide all over the affected area and gently worked out most of the dirt and gravel. I slathered him in Neosporin ointment and applied a no-stick bandage, all without his feeling a thing!

Freeze it then clean it. By gently freezing the skin around a minor injury, you can freeze the pain away long enough to get an initial treatment going and find out how serious things are going to be.

60

MY BIG FAT *ICY* GREEK WEDDING

There is a wonderful film called *My Big Fat Greek Wedding*.

The father in that film, played by Michael Constantine, had a solution for almost everything: Windex. No matter how large or small the problem, Windex somehow figured into the solution. Dirty windows, a white dress with a big smudge, shoe marks on the tile floor? Of course, Windex. Sometimes he just sprayed it in the air to celebrate.

My Windex is ice. No matter what else it does for your injured child, ice does something immediately, and it rarely does harm. There is always room for ice in the equation if a parent or coach or elder is trying to make a little one feel better after a minor injury.

Ice is an excellent first step, an easy beginning to any efforts directed at healing or helping your daughter. Ice provides her with the satisfaction that you did listen to her and that something is being done *right away*.

For most bumps and bruises, muscle pulls and muscle strains, a bag of ice or a cold pack can be applied directly to the injured area. Try two minutes on, then two minutes off. Repeat if necessary. You can use this time to dry tears and listen to her side of the story. And then get her back in the game or activity as soon as possible.

Ice reduces most early swelling and allows you to investigate the injury and determine if more is required than basic kindness.

The use of ice is most valuable and effective in the first twenty-four hours, since any minor damage to the muscle or skin is set after that point and the effectiveness of ice is much reduced thereafter.

For cuts and scrapes, especially where you will be required to clean her up and remove dirt and debris, apply the ice generously all around the injury and freeze out any topical sensation by inching closer and closer (see "Freeze It / Then Clean It" for more details).

It may be that ice is required around a tricky angle, such as a knuckle or a big toe. Keep an extra bag of peas in the freezer and use it for this purpose. The bag is very flexible and can get more coldness into smaller spaces.

When in doubt, start with some ice. Much more effective than Windex.

61

THE GROUND IS ON FIRE

It is inevitable that children are going to fall down at some point in a contest, and the more hotly contested the match or game is, the greater the likelihood. Whether via a bump or a trip, a stumble or a push, children will find themselves lying on the gym floor or the field.

A man I know who works very well with children has created an excellent aphorism to get them back on their feet right away.

Dimitri Upshaw runs a basketball program for young children in Manhattan Beach, California. He is also head referee and referee trainer for Manhattan Beach Youth Basketball.

His classes are friendly, supportive, and instructive, and the children hear many of the same ideas that they will hear at any basketball camp. Run harder, pass better, play better defense, look for the open man, etc. But they also hear a message that they have never heard before in any other camp.

He does not let his athletes linger when they go down. There is no break in the action just because they lost their footing or tripped. Once he determines that the injury is not too serious, Dimitri shouts out that *the ground is on fire!* In other words, they are just making it worse by staying down there. Their butts are starting to melt, their hands are starting to burn. He says the longer you stay down, the harder it will be to get up when you do get up.

So the athletes muster their courage and get back up on their feet, snuffle away the pain, shake hands with the one who made them fall, and play on.

When children get hurt playing, they often receive more attention than if they actually did something heroic. Parents rush over, gushing, cellphones at the ready, ambulances on call somewhere. They smother their children and ultimately teach an entirely incorrect lesson. If athletes get just as much attention for a fall or a stumble as for their athletic prowess, the wrong message is being sent. While the kindness is well intentioned, too much of it actually encourages children to stay hurt, stay down, and stay on the ground.

Sports is about getting back on your feet, staying in the game until the end, finding the passion and meaning, playing with all your heart, even with a little injury, and never giving up and never giving in to anyone.

Let your children believe that the ground is on fire, that they should never find themselves lying down while their teammates are waiting for them to get back up. Let them know that they *will* get the wind knocked out of them sometimes, both literally and figuratively—at school, in life, any time, anywhere.

They have to learn to get back up and get back in the game. It is the only way to move forward in this contest or any other contest that might be run.

The ground is on fire is a principle to live by.

#62

SQUEEZE MY HAND
AS MUCH AS IT HURTS

In those first few minutes after an injury, children are often shocked and surprised by how much they are hurting. Maybe they do not yet understand how well their central nervous system operates. Maybe they are asking themselves how one little cut or scrape can hurt that much.

One way to communicate with them while they are still in the throes of the pain and tears is to have them tell you how much it hurts. Understandably, words cannot begin to express it in some cases, and with all of the crying and wailing that might be going on, words might not be available.

Let them speak without words. Put your hand (or finger) in theirs, and ask them to squeeze as much as it hurts. This is one way they can begin to communicate to you some measure of the pain they are feeling.

Your understanding is a very important component of their healing.

No matter how hard they squeeze, be surprised that it hurts *that* much, because somehow—and I am not sure how exactly—the act of communicating how much pain they are in begins to ease that pain. For some reason it hurts just a little less once children have communicated to their parents the full extent of their injuries.

When you let children squeeze your hand or finger to demonstrate the amount of pain they are feeling, you will show them your compassion and understanding of their plight. You will show them that you are both sympathetic and empathetic to their painful situation. You will show them that you comprehend the injury and feel their pain with them.

Let them squeeze your hand to show you how much it hurts (and be surprised!).

63

DO NOT RUSH TO END THE TEARS

So often a parent's first reaction to the sight of a crying child is to tell the child to stop crying. But for the most part, crying is an involuntary act, especially if brought on by some minor injury, whether emotional or physical.

There is just no stopping it sometimes.

Parents want the crying to stop right away because it is embarrassing to stand there, helplessly, while a child wails away right next to you. It's a little like standing next to a human air raid siren. Strangers stop and stare. Other children point, as if one of their own is being mistreated. It occurs to you that passersby might think that you are not such a great parent after all.

You might catch yourself saying, "Okay, that's enough," "Grow up and stop crying, Mister," "Big girls don't cry, Eunice," "Now you're just making a scene," "There's no crying in baseball," and so forth.

But what's the rush?

When your son is hurt and crying, it is okay to coo in his ear and let him know that it will all be okay in a little while. Let him work it out for a minute or two. Throw your arms around him and comfort him completely. He will be done soon enough.

There is nothing embarrassing about showing a child love

when he needs it the most, particularly at the time when he needs *you* the most.

Try being completely sympathetic and understanding. Say that you wish it were you hurting, and not him. Say that you would trade places with him if you could. Say that you saw the whole thing and that it was not his fault at all. Say that you would be crying too if it happened to you.

This is not an ideal moment to share your vast wisdom. It's not a great time to pick any low-hanging fruit from the tree of knowledge. His tears are not the cue for you to throw around a good "I told you this would happen, Jarvis. . . ."

When your son is crying, just hold him in your arms. Let him know what complete protection feels like. Hug him and let him cry it out. There should be no rush to end the tears.

64

HOW TO PUT OUT A FIRE, RED ADAIR-STYLE

Red Adair was one of the most daring men in the world. "Fearless" would not begin to describe this native Texan and his ability to restore order in the midst of complete chaos and panic. Where others faltered, he took a deep breath, gathered his forces around him, and regained control of situations that were completely out of control.

Red Adair was the best ever at putting out oil well fires. Red extinguished fires that were so big and so impossible to fight, they had their own names!

He put out the Piper Alpha fire on a platform rig in the North Sea, braving eighty-mile-per-hour winds and seventy-foot swells! He put out the Devil's Cigarette Lighter in the Sahara—a fire that had burned for six months while shooting a torch of flame into the air 450 feet high. He was the man who was called into Kuwait to contain the 117 oil well fires that Iraqi troops ignited in 1991 after their failed invasion.

Red understood that fire needs oxygen to live, and big fires need ridiculous amounts of oxygen. His techniques varied, but they all came down to the same principle: Deny a fire the oxygen it thirsts for, and you have conquered it.

He might pour truckloads of cement down a burning well, or drown a fire in millions of gallons of sea water, but the technique that he was most famous for was his use of dynamite. He would carefully position a charge of dynamite very near the heart of the fire, and then ignite it. The result was that, for just a couple of seconds, the blast separated the fire from its oxygen, its fuel. In the fire's confusion, he would race in and cap the well.

Sometimes a child can burn like an oil well fire. He can rage along, completely inconsiderate of anything or anyone trying to stop him. He can devour vast amounts of your resources, energy, and time in the meantime.

It might be a crying jag, or a temper tantrum, or a mean streak, or maybe he is just being ill mannered that particular day.

It happens in the best families.

You, the parent or elder, must regain control of the situation, or lose an entire day or afternoon to this nonsense. You must force your will on the circumstances and change his behavior just long enough to take back the direction of the day. You must disrupt and distract, and in the confusion that ensues, reestablish your authority.

Your attention is the oxygen. His tantrum is the fire. The two must be separated long enough to break the chain of events and restore order.

The dynamite that will do this, that will confuse and separate your child from his nasty habit, is water, a few drops of water, whether flicked from your fingertips or shot at him from a turkey baster, or a water pistol you keep hidden but handy.

Catch a ranting child in the back of the head with a good squirt of water that runs down his neck, and everything changes. It will be nearly impossible for him to keep up a good vent while

154

he is trying to figure out what's dripping down his shirt. A gentle flick of water in the face will have the same disruptive and distracting (and harmless) effect.

Be ready to seize the opportunity and cap the well. Have the next activity ready to go, and when the moment comes, seize it. Be ready to jump to the next thing, and then jump to it. Before your child has time to remember that he was in the middle of a rant/cry/tantrum, he is in the car on the way to the store, or playing catch, or watching a movie.

Distract and conquer. Disrupt the pattern and change the agenda. Regain control of the day. Move on quickly and decisively. Separate your son from his runaway tears, his tantrum from its fuel. Separate the flame from the oxygen.

Put out the fire, Red Adair–style.

Chapter 7
PLAY SPORTS, PERIOD

Sports provide one of the greatest opportunities for parents to spend rewarding and fulfilling time with their children.

Playing sports is exercise, conversation, socializing, strategizing, sunshine, and a real chance to start planning and planting big dreams. Sports is a regimen of things for you to do with your children without their even "knowing" that you are doing anything at all. It is the development of eye-hand coordination and other physical skills. Having your child participate in sports is one of the most practical, enjoyable, and immediately impactful ways that you can influence their lives for the better.

Learning how to play sports—and how to win and lose—is nearly as important as learning how to read and speak. Sports will help define how children play adult games when they grow up.

Sports show children what passion looks like, as they watch you root for them or your favorite team. Sports teach children what dreams are made of, as they cheer on a favorite college or pro player who achieves a hard-fought championship. Children see determination and grit in action, as when a boxer gets up off the canvas to successfully defend his belt.

Success in sports is a measure of passion and dreams and will and determination. It is a measure of how far someone will go in pursuit of his or her soul's fulfillment.

The sooner your children feel and see sports interact with their lives, and see this magical coalescence in action, the better they will understand their own dreams once those begin to appear and bloom.

There are many lessons that children will learn about the life that awaits them through the sports they play now.

How will they handle a moment of triumph? Will they learn to be gracious winners? Can they learn to play as a member of a team regardless of the outcome of the match? Or will they blame the ref and howl about a bad call all the way home?

Playing alongside you or watching you as you enjoy your favorite sports, your children will see you in difficult moments as well. They will be watching to see how you react, and interact with victory or loss. How you handle your winning and losing moments will be the lesson that you teach them as to how to handle theirs. Good or bad, gracious or ignoble, your actions and reactions will be imprinted on them forever.

How to play sports provides children with a basic template for how to play at life.

The following are some ideas on how to introduce, balance, and maintain fair and fun sports in your children's lives.

TEAM SPORTS? SIGN 'EM UP

When Thomas was five years old, we attended a birthday party at the pagoda in Polliwog Park in Manhattan Beach when Richard Frank showed up with his daughter, Lauren. I had never seen a child look so resplendent. Talk about glamorous—she looked ready to defend the World Cup, as if she just stepped out of a sports equipment catalog.

She was wearing a bright-purple-striped jersey, black shorts, and bright purple socks. On the back of the jersey was a huge white 7. Her hair was pulled back with a matching color-coordinated purple scrunchie. Her cleats clattered on the wood floor like Fred Astaire crossing to the bar in *Top Hat*. It was pretty fantastic.

I looked at Richard and pointed to Lauren. "What's all that?" I said.

As though answering what two plus two equals, he said, "It's AYSO." I had never heard the acronym before but soon learned that she was on a team in the American Youth Soccer Organization, a community of young soccer athletes.

It turned out that participants got uniforms, referees, painted fields, teammates, and, at the end of the year, trophies! It was perfect—exactly what a parent would hope to bring to his child.

Thomas was close by, so I asked him if he wanted to play soccer like Lauren. He said, "No, I don't think so, Dad."

I signed him up the next day.

I wanted him to have a uniform with a big number on the back, and the socks to match, and big loud shoes that scratch the floor, and the weekly buildup to the big game, and the chance to score goals and hang out with his teammates. The whole beautiful scenario had already unfolded in my mind like a million dominoes stretching down a deserted highway.

But Thomas could not have known all of this, or all of the benefits. How could he have known? There was no way that he could make an informed decision. So I made the decision for him, and we never looked back. He played soccer for eight seasons, made several all-star teams, was a champion a few times, learned the joy of winning and the pain of losing, and while he was at it, became a very capable and powerful athlete, and had a great time most of the time.

But he would never have known any of this if I had let *him* make the decision. What child will agree to do anything when he does not know what it is, where it takes place, when it happens, or how it impacts him exactly?

In Thomas's world, the future was lunch. Long-term planning was later that afternoon. Big picture? He just wanted to know what was for dinner. The next week was a foggy light way off in the distance somewhere. How could he have possibly understood the meaning of words like *season* or *commitment*?

No child will say, "Why yes, I'd love to do that, Father . . ." when he has no idea what "that" is exactly.

At the first opportunity, sign your child up for any organized team sport. Basketball or soccer or baseball—just sign him up.

Do not ask any questions, do not take a temperature on it, and do not wonder if it is the right thing to do. It is the right thing to do. After a season or two he will figure out if it is a good sport for him or not. But in the meantime, he will learn the complex joy of team sports.

Make the decision for your children when they cannot make an informed decision themselves. When there is a chance to play a team sport, sign 'em up.

66

GAME DAY / NEXT DAY

One of the most unfortunate things to see at the conclusion of a children's sporting event is a disappointed parent or coach challenging, scolding, or unloving a child on the way to the parking lot, or lecturing her on the long drive home.

The parent is clearly unhappy with the outcome of the contest, or the quality of effort put forth by the child, or the fact that somebody maybe got a little distracted standing out there in the hot sun all afternoon.

What must it be like for the girl in this situation? She gave all she had, left it all on the field, tried her hardest, and for what? She is hot and sweating and trapped in the backseat of the car, and all she wants is a little sip of cold water, some appreciation, and some understanding. But all she gets is disappointed commentary and a walk-through of her multiple mistakes.

Though it might be somewhat well intentioned, this behavior is not fair, not kind, not loving, and might not be great parenting. Do not bring your child any unhappiness at all after a sporting event. Employ the Game Day / Next Day rule.

On game day, treat her like a star. Let her be the champion of the house. This is her reward for all the practices and effort leading up to this contest. Getting ready for the game, she is your very own Michael Jordan, Roger Clemens, Maria Sharapova, or Holly McPeak.

After the game, let her feel amazing about what she just accomplished. Okay, so it was not the greatest moment in the long history of eight-year-old girls' basketball. Let her have her moment in the sun anyway. Let her know the feeling of your complete admiration, total support, and absolute belief.

Let your praise and her sweat mix into a cocktail of champions that she will want to taste again and again. Let the rush of adrenaline from the game, and the cool wash of your recognition afterward, become part of another perfect day.

Irrespective of a win or a loss, simply by playing she has earned the right to your complete respect, and praise is only meaningful when it is *unconditional!*

The next day, everything is back to normal. She is back to being your daughter again; the rebalance has been achieved. Now is the time to offer some well-thought-out commentary or criticism on her play the previous day.

By this time, you will have had a chance to distill your message and arrive at a few key bullet points, instead of a lecture that lasts the drive home and stretches into the rest of the afternoon or weekend.

Also, this way you can calm down and recover your flagging decorum, especially if the game was part of a tournament or a championship, and double-especially if your child was the athlete most responsible for a loss.

The Game Day / Next Day rule shows your daughter that you appreciate and respect the effort that she puts forth trying to be your champion, regardless of the outcome of the contest.

67

COACHING IS A PRIVILEGE

My friend Robert gave up his athletic career in the ninth grade when he got run over by a bad coach. It was Little League and he was a boy of summer, or at least he was trying to be. He hustled and sweated, ran out every grounder, chased down the balls hit over his head, and gave 110 percent in every drill and exercise and game. But it was never quite enough for Mr. F.

His coach, a former high school player, berated and chided, grumped and grumbled, discouraged and diminished, and gradually wore down Robert's will to play baseball until he wore it all away. One day, Robert had had enough.

After practice, he put away his glove and never picked it up again.

Many years later, when he told me this story, I could see that it still bothered him, and I could see why. He never got to fulfill that part of his life's dream, and the coach that prevented him from doing so was still a part of his life, was still remembered, but for all the wrong reasons.

Coaching is one of the best opportunities available to be a positive influence, to guide and mentor and challenge, and to reward and nourish development in a child. But coaches of young athletes must be ever aware of the impact that they can have on the psyches of the children whose lives are entrusted to them.

Coaches must step carefully around the dreams, hopes, and infinite possibilities that children use to decorate their hearts when imagining and dreaming of their futures.

Coaching is a privilege.

I have coached twelve teams so far, either as assistant or as the head coach.

My coaching is probably not like that of most coaches, and I think that my athletes like to play for me because of it. I respect them all the more because I have *not* done what I am asking them to do. I can only imagine what it must be like to be talented and athletic.

In the sports that I love to coach, I have no practical experience whatsoever, and many of the athletes on these teams have more talent and ability at the age of seven than I have now or probably ever did have. I have never hoisted the champion's trophy, never made the last-minute shot that won the big game, or the bone-jarring tackle that stopped the other team in a fourth-and-one situation. I never had my teammates turn to me with a couple of ticks left on the old gym clock and say, "If anybody can do it, you can, Tom. We're counting on you." But that lack of experience does not limit me—it ennobles me.

Here are my six principles of good coaching:

1. Athletes have to try their hardest until the very last second of every game, regardless of the apparent or even likely outcome. No quitting, ever.
2. Winning or losing is not as important as how well the players played, and how hard they tried.
3. Good sportsmanship must be shown at every opportunity. Being a good sport provides the foundation for how to live

a good life. Knocked someone down? Help them right up. Shake hands with every player at the end of the game. That kind of thing . . .

4. The team is more valuable and important than any individual player on it.
5. Every child should play in every game.
6. But overriding all of these: Coaches have a sacred duty to their players to ensure that every season, every child has his or her best sports experience. This is the most important thing that a coach can bring to a team and the players on it.

To accomplish this last and most important goal, it should be the coach's first challenge to help each child set, understand, and work hard to meet an individual goal. A skilled child athlete will have much different goals than a beginner or less skilled player on the same team. One soccer child may be trying to perfect a bicycle kick while another is just hoping to get his first goal. A young girl may be hoping that she can just learn to dribble a basketball this year while her teammate is already knocking down three-pointers.

If you want to make a difference in a child's life, become a coach. But become a good coach, a respecting coach, an inspiring coach. Years later, your athletes may or may not remember you, but if they do, let it be for all the right reasons.

THE ESPN RULE

My son Sam is a gifted athlete. Near the end of a game, when everything is on the line and his team needs a goal, or a basket, or a home run, or a touchdown, his confidence soars and he shines. He seeks out the moment and he lives for it. He has the capacity to rise to the occasion and give his 100 percent effort.

Sometimes it all works out perfectly. The shot he puts up in a basketball game goes through the hoop just as the buzzer sounds, or the soccer ball he kicks does just get over the out-stretched hand of the keeper and forces the game into OT. Or a ten-foot putt does just roll in on the eighteenth green and wins the match for his golf team.

But not all the time does it go so perfectly.

I have heard the clank of the basketball off the back of the rim when Sam missed a big shot. I have heard myself say, "Uh-oh . . ." when a player on the opposing soccer team faked him out of his spikes to shoot a goal. I have watched him take three putts to get across a green, and lose the chance to break ninety for the first time. But he keeps trying. He keeps believing. He rarely doubts. He has no fear of failure. Every time he competes he believes he will succeed. He has built up a momentum of confidence that carries him into every day, every game, every match, every sport-ing event.

I believe this confidence will carry him forward into his adulthood, and help to shape and define the man that he will become.

One of the best ways to give your child confidence in himself is to have complete confidence in *him*. Celebrate his successes, and lead him to believe that it can and will happen again and again. What is confidence, after all, but a belief that anything is possible?

Confidence is the magic factor that separates champions from the rest of the players on the field. Confidence is the residue of always trying your hardest, always giving your all.

Give your children confidence by reminding them just how good you think they are. One way to accomplish this is through the ESPN Rule.

ESPN made the brilliant discovery that reporting on sports is much more dramatic and interesting when the story of the game is being told, not simply the score. ESPN allows its viewers to relive the drama of the match and its significance by defining the arc of the characters within it, and how they responded in the crucible of competition.

Use this template to build in your child a belief that there is nothing that he cannot do. The next time the family is getting together, or even when it is just you and him out somewhere, tell the story of his most recent sporting success. Become your children's very own private ESPN announcer.

I have seen the most beautiful smile creep across Sam's face when I begin to tell a story about something amazing that he did. He relives the story as he hears it being told. I include quotes from bystanders, commentary of the other parents, the significance of the officiating, the ticking of the clock down to one second left—every detail is vital.

It is excellent parenting to remind your child that he has achieved something remarkable and that you are proud of him. This will let him know the sweet taste of your approval. You will also be providing him with the basis of an aura of invincibility that he can utilize in the next contest, and the next, and the next. This growing confidence will become a factor in his play and quite possibly in his life.

One caveat: Tell the story of his heroic efforts over and over, but not for too long. If you are telling the same tale months later, and another exploit has not come along to replace it, it will become less of a highlight of his life and more of an albatross around his neck.

Second caveat: The ESPN Rule applies to telling the story of *any* accomplishment, whether educational, social, creative, or sports-oriented.

69

COMPLETE VICTORIES

My dear friend Dan has a daughter, Valentina. She is beautiful and musical, has long brown hair, and loves to dance. For a dance recital one year for third grade, she invites everyone she knows, and she is stupendous. Leaping and turning, jumping and spinning. Just extraordinary.

We all stand backstage to congratulate and praise her for her remarkable performance, and she is soaking it in. Then my friend Dan, her father, chooses this particular moment, in front of everyone, to let her know that her leg could have been a little straighter at the top of a difficult kick, and reminds her that she lost her balance during a particular pirouette. He closes by telling her, "But it was very close to fantastic."

I do not need to look at her face to feel the heartbreak that she feels. I feel it for her, as does everyone else in the group. We jump to praise her even more, but it is too late. Her victory is taken from her. A potentially triumphant moment is denied her.

She blinks her way through tears of embarrassment. She is brave and smiles at us. Right there in front of everyone she grows up a little too fast.

It is vital for every child to feel that she can win the *complete* approval of her parents and mentors and coaches, that she can have complete victories, and that it is possible to get praise without a preface, rewards without reductions, and compliments without conditions.

A well-meaning parent can defeat a child's will by choosing the exact moment of exultation to offer a pointed criticism, or faint praise, or to introduce a new and even more difficult challenge.

A daughter will lead her team to a victory in a basketball game, but her coach will remind her that she sank only one of six from the free throw line. A son will receive an A on a paper about Socrates, and then have to field graduate-school-level questions about Homer or Thucydides. Or maybe a dancer does not get her leg quite straight enough at the top of a kick.

Give your daughter the satisfaction of earning your unconditional praise. Let her come to know the sheer joy of hearing your unedited adulation.

Allow her victories to be complete.

MANDATORY ATTENDANCE

The Rules are very clear on this point—no matter what, why, or how, parents should try to attend every organized league game that their children play. Every single one. If the child is wearing a uniform, the parent should be there to see it.

No excuses are acceptable, short of an extended hospital stay or possibly front-row seats to see Tony Bennett sing *Don Giovanni* at the Met.

The more that sports matter to the parents, the more that sports will matter to the children. The more that sports matter to the children, the more they will get out of them. The more they get out of sports, the more sports will influence and benefit their young lives.

Think of your attendance at their games as yet another opportunity for you to show your children that you love them as no parent has ever loved a child.

THE CARRYOVER OF
THE UNREALIZED DREAM

There is one particular soccer coach I have watched in amazement over several years of playing against him. He literally screams at his team (and his son in particular) all game long.

I spoke with him after an event once, and inquired about his own career in sports. Turned out he was *almost* a soccer star. He came very close. He now believes that if he had just worked harder, practiced longer, gotten up earlier, and wanted it more than all of the other guys did, somehow things would have turned out differently for him.

But now he is fifty-plus pounds heavier and unaccepting of the fact that maybe he was just not quite good enough when he was younger and it was his turn. His dream went unrealized and now he takes it with him everywhere he goes, like a pet.

He gets his son up earlier, and makes him work harder, and sweats every defeat like it *is* the end of the world. He only celebrates a victory if it is a really big game. Without meaning to, he denies himself and his son the magic of sports: a chance to be together and to have fun together.

The message that his son gets is that there is no pleasing his father and that there is never enough that can be done. Sooner or later, his son may disconnect from soccer or sports altogether and move on to other pursuits, creating even greater distance between him and his well-intentioned father.

The coach seemed unable to forgive himself. Maybe he hoped that his child's success would wipe clean the slate, and wipe out the memory of his own athletic disappointments. And that may or may not happen, but why would he risk his son's childhood trying to find out?

The son has his own big dreams to imagine and his own life to live. The journey will be hard enough without the awkward ballast of his father's unwieldy expectations and unrealized dream to carry along as well.

72

ADJUST THE LEVEL OF DIFFICULTY

In almost all the video games out now, there is an adjustment that can make each game harder or easier, depending on the quality of challenge the player is looking for.

In Madden Football, for instance, the level of difficulty has four settings: Rookie, Pro, All-Pro, and All Star. In Gears of War, the levels are Casual, Hardcore, and Insane. In Fight Night, the settings are Amateur, Professional, and Legendary. And in Halo, the most popular video game in the world, there are four choices: Easy, Normal, Legendary, and Heroic.

The adjustment of the level of difficulty lets players enjoy any video game at the degree of competence where they are most comfortable. It gives them control, lets them play at their skill level, and allows them to get more enjoyment out of the experience.

This is a great guideline for parents playing with children. Let children adjust *your* level of difficulty and make any game they play with you more fun for them.

Whatever the game, ask your children how hard they want you to play. Not in a challenging or bullying way—just ask and give them control of the moment, and more fun, more to laugh about later.

You can offer a menu of levels to choose from. Level 1 would be no resistance whatsoever. Level 2 would give them a sporting chance to beat you if they try really hard. Level 3 would mean that the game is probably going to be over in the first thirty seconds because you are going to crunch their dunch (figuratively speaking, of course).

You might tell them that Level 4 is how hard you play against your friends, and they will only be able to imagine how hard you play on Level 5.

Let your children adjust all aspects of the level of difficulty of their playtime with you. Then adjust your game to suit the challenge that will be most enjoyable for them, not you. This element of control will give them one more reason to love playing with you, and against you.

73

THE TAP-TAP RULE

The Ultimate Fighting Championship is a grisly sport pitting two men against each other in a fight to the bitter end. The end comes when one of the combatants "taps out." He does this by tapping his flat hand twice on any surface: the mat, the fence, the opponent's back, wherever. The referee is always looking for this motion to signal the end of the match.

Once the player "taps out," the fight is over, instantly. There is no question of the outcome, and there is no commentary from either side. It is over.

Wrestling, child-boxing, living room football, or just general roughhousing can get very rough very quickly for the smaller ones in the game. They are desperate to be included but can easily get tossed around or trampled underfoot.

The adults or older children might not recognize that a little one has gotten himself into a difficult position at the bottom of the pile in a football or rugby scrum, or simply might not be having fun anymore. Maybe that game of Speed Twister got a little too rough for him and he wants out.

The Tap-Tap Rule is the great equalizer.

Let your son know that he has the right to call out "Tap-tap!" any time, anywhere, in any situation. The game, whatever it is, stops instantly, right then and right there, no questions asked. It is like rebooting a computer or pulling the plug on a video game: game over.

The Tap-Tap Rule works well in any game that you play with your son. It gives him back some control over the contest and the right to say when he has had enough.

Knowing that he has an option will give your son more room and freedom to enjoy himself in any physical circumstance where things can get out of hand at a moment's notice.

The Tap-Tap Rule can be used in other situations as well, and might become one of your son's tools to let you know he is not having fun anymore—whether at school, the dinner table, or watching you shop for some new drill bits at the hardware store.

Tap-tap. It's over.

74

NO DARES

Airplane pilots have a saying: "There are old pilots, and there are daring pilots, but there are no old daring pilots."

This simple apothegm contains applicable wisdom for good parenting. In your child's world, a dare should be as recognizable as an airplane.

A dare is the ugly little challenge made by one child to another, most often by an older child to a younger one, a larger child to a smaller one, a cunning child to a naïve one, or a bullying child to a bullied one, and is usually made just out of earshot of the adult who could stop the whole ugly exchange from taking place.

The smaller/younger/naïve child is given the opportunity to prove that he is not "chicken" or that he "has the guts" to do something stupid, foolish, or risky. The older/larger/smarter child has planted this idea in the younger child's head as a momentary and often cruel amusement. The darer is too smart to take the risk himself, or too scared, and undoubtedly could not care less about the dangerous outcome.

Both sides lose no matter how you look at it. Every dare is a bad idea, and there is no such thing as a good dare.

A dare requires *two* fools: one to propose and one to accept. Try not to let your child be either one.

If your child has gotten into the habit of issuing dares, this is a habit worth losing. Maybe it all seems rather innocent now, but there is no good that can come of it later.

On the other hand, if your child is the naïve one, the "dare-ee," teach him to recognize the empty promises inherent in a dare. And, when one is presented, teach him to enjoy the pleasure of simply walking away from it. No dare is worth the risk, ever.

No dares, please.

75

ANY GAME/ANY TIME

The need for an excellent game can pop up at any moment, sometimes quite suddenly and often when you are least expecting it.

Thanksgiving: the football games are over, the dinner is finished, and nobody will be leaving for a very long time. What to do with all that time and all those people? Or Super Bowl Sunday. Your guests and their children came over early to beat the traffic, just as you suggested. Now what? Or, it's your child's birthday and Lucky the Party Clown is calling from a liquor store asking if you are willing to pay a gasoline surcharge while twenty-five children stare up at you and wonder how you intend to entertain them in the meanwhile.

What does one do? How do you whip together an interesting contest out of thin air? Where do you find a test of skills or wills that can challenge a nine-year-old and her nineteen-year-old cousin? A match that can accommodate five, ten, or twenty participants? One that stays interesting, with lots of drama and a big finish?

There are four ingredients that can turn almost any gathering—regardless of the ages or abilities of the children or adults involved—into a game:

PARKING LOT RULES

A COMPETITION—Football, basketball, soccer, spelling, cooking, designing new buildings, dictionary, team chess or team Scrabble, twenty questions—whatever thrills you, anything that allows sides to be chosen. Once you decide on the game, decide on some basic, easy-to-follow rules, but freely modify and adjust the parameters to fit the group that is playing.

A SCOREBOARD—Keep score, no matter what the game is. Scoring is how you keep everyone interested, and how children get to measure their success against the others in the game. There should be more points for successful attempts, fewer points for unsuccessful attempts, but always points for something, with extra points for any play that involves the youngest players.

HANDICAPS—Adjust the competition and its rules so that younger players have a distinct advantage, as this alone ensures a level playing field. Maybe the younger players get to stand closer to the basket, or putt from closer to the hole. Or they have to spell *cat* instead of *chrysanthemum*. Whatever the game, it has to be easier for the younger players to achieve the same points as the older players.

A BIG FINISH—Before the game begins, determine how it will end, whether as a result of time, points, mercy rule, penalty kicks, sudden-death challenge, or a coin toss. Let your players know at the beginning exactly how the game will end.

Caveats, adjustments, fine tunings, and quid pro quos:

1. Play short games, not long ones. Think Keno—a new game every seven minutes.

2. Pick new teams for every new game.
3. You, the referee/announcer, have final say on all rulings.

Reenactments of great sporting events can be amazing templates for any game, any time. The 1987 Cotton Bowl or the 2005 Rose Bowl for football. Lakers versus Detroit in the 2004 NBA Finals for basketball. Boris Spassky versus Bobby Fischer for chess-club types.

All that an imaginative parent should need to get any game going at any time are these four elements: a well-defined competition, a scoreboard with lots of points, handicaps to help out the littler ones, and a big dramatic finish.

COURAGE AND ENCOURAGEMENT

Thomas's fifth-grade soccer team was called the Hurricanes. I was the coach but Thomas was running the team with me. It was one of the greatest childhood father-son experiences that I have ever known with him. He and I would strategize for every game, design the defense, and decide the responsibilities of the other players.

It was an amazing year. The team went undefeated over a ten-game season. Thomas was one of the youngest players but was a league leader in goals scored, and a true captain on the field. He played harder than anyone else and directed the other players where to go and when to go there.

The Hurricanes made it as far as the semifinal playoff game, a match against the league commissioner's team. From the first moments of the contest, it was clear that we were going to be outcoached, and it was obvious that he knew what he was doing and just as obvious that I did not. My luck had finally run out.

The teams battled fiercely, but with only minutes left, we were down 2–0.

And though the season was lost, and clearly the championship would not be ours, Thomas absolutely refused to give up. He showed strength of courage that I never knew he had. Again and again he forced the issue, bringing the ball up against a well-coached and patient defense that would not let him through to score.

Finally, with just seconds left in the game, he looked over at me, his dad and his coach. His hands were on his hips, and his mouth was open, gasping for air. He was strong to the end, losing but not beaten, bowed but not broken. Mud streaked his face. Our eyes met and he shook his head from side to side, as if to say, "Okay, *now* it's over . . ."

I flashed him back the hand sign "I love you," hoping to say that nothing mattered more than that, that my belief in him was limitless, and that the score was insignificant compared with the lesson that he had just taught me about what kind of boy he was.

Courage is a seed that can be planted in the fertile ground of a child's believing heart. It can be grown and nurtured and harvested.

Courage is overcoming fear of failing. It is believing that victory is still possible, even against impossible odds. Courage is losing the game but playing every minute and every second anyway. Courage is wanting the ball with virtually no time left when the team needs a desperation shot just to tie.

Your children look to you, their parent or elder, as their first true believer. You are their first fan. If you think that they can do something, then they think they can, too. Believing is contagious. The more you believe in your children, the more they will believe in themselves.

Out of your encouragement grow the seeds of their courage. But your belief and encouragement must be unconditional. They must be unwavering. They must be unchangeable and immutable.

Your child athlete must know in his heart that the outcome of any match or contest is secondary to your love and understanding, your belief in his ability. The score does not reflect his skills, only the results of a particular contest.

We are what we repeatedly do, says Aristotle. Encouraging our children at every chance, in every game, on every field and court, will enable their courage to take root, grow, and blossom.

Like excellence, courage, too, can become a habit.

Coda

Just a few nights ago, after basketball practice, I put Sam in the tub. I was just starting to clean up his room, put away his toys, organize his books for homework, and get ready for the rest of his evening when I heard him shout to me from the bathroom: "Hey, Dad, get in here please! Remember, this is the best time to talk to your child!" After I stopped laughing, I read him some books and we discussed the possibility of his becoming the first athlete to play in the PGA and in the NBA simultaneously, and some of his other big dreams.

I describe this moment simply because it is the essence of the Parking Lot Rules, the microcosm that illustrates the macrocosm, the single rose that proves the whole garden is healthy and beautiful.

The Rules were not holding him back or preventing him from doing something. Rather, he was using them to his benefit, to improve a moment, to make a great day perfect. He was using the Rules just as they were intended to be used.

The Parking Lot Rules are meant to make the world a better place for you and your children, to provide more opportunities for you to communicate, and to encourage you to frame your interactions with them always in love and kindness.

The Rules can give your children options that they can utilize when they need you, whether to play with them, talk with them, dream with them, or simply just to notice that they are in the same room trying to tell you a story.

I said in the beginning that it is impossible to show a child too much respect but worth the effort to try, and I believe this is central to raising amazing children. Children should be our everything, and our responsibility as their parents, family, coaches, mentors, or teachers is clear. Respect them always and forever, in every circumstance, every day. The higher the arc of respect that our children know growing up, the greater their journey through life will be.

Acknowledgments

The journey that started with scratching out a few ideas on the back of an envelope and led to actually publishing a book was much longer than I could ever have imagined. I needed the guidance and wisdom and generosity of many people along the way.

Karen Otto: This book does not exist without you. Your understanding and mastery of the technology of this process allowed me the time and freedom to turn hundreds of notes and turns of phrase into ideas, themes, essays, chapters, and, ultimately, a manuscript. Your insights are everywhere here. I treasure and thank you for this gift. Tlhk.

Susan Raihofer: I had heard so much about you and the David Black Agency, and it turns out that your team is as remarkable as I had been told. Thank you for agreeing to represent me, and for helping me to get the book ready for its pitch to the book-publishing community. You are the consummate professional and a most reliable partner in this adventure.

Libby McGuire, Christina Duffy, Jane von Mehren, Cindy Murray, Christine Cabello, Kim Hovey, Janet Wygal, and all my Random House teammates: From our first meeting on, you all have been generous with your time, wisdom, knowledge, dedication, and professionalism. I am very grateful for the chance to be working with you.

Dina LaPolt, Linda Newmark, Kris Munoz, Denise Marsa, and Justin Loeber: You are the delicate human chain that led me from being "Person with Manuscript" to being "Author with Agent," through literally five degrees of separation. Your willingness to share your friends and contacts was extraordinary. Justin, you were particularly generous in helping me, and I am very grateful to you.

Dr. Eli Lieber, respected researcher, parent, coach, husband, giver-to-your-community: Thank you for taking time from your many schedules to write the Foreword.

Shaquille O'Neal, Brad Arnold, and Carole Bayer Sager: You were kind enough to provide blurbs for shopping the book. Thank you for your early belief in my gentle cause.

Regina Boutte, Patricia Ware, Jennifer Parker, and Alyse McDonald: You are four of the most dedicated and gifted educators I have ever met. Thank you for allowing me to mentor, teach, and volunteer with hundreds of your students, and to put into practice the idea that respecting children *too* much is impossible.

Michael Rexford: Your copyediting and other insights are most appreciated, and I am thankful for your contributions.

Jeff Gelb: Your valuable encouragements on a very early draft provided much important guidance, and I probably would not be here without them.

Dani Lopez: Your simple comment that you do not think of your daughter as a kid but rather as a child changed the tone and patina of many essays.

Kim and Scott Fisher: Your insistence that one of my stories quite simply did not belong turned out to be prescient and wise counsel—and farewell forever to those few drops of ink.

Robert and Susan Allen: You allowed me to borrow from your

life for Coaching Is a Privilege, and then doubled the favor with thorough readings and well-thought-out suggestions and ideas.

Austin Chavira and Shawn Driz: Your willingness to trust in Kids Court allowed a friendship and confirms that rule's value as a conflict-resolution tool for children of any age.

Deirdre O'Hara, Jena Markey, Lauren Young, Rebecca Wright, Lindsey Lanier, Allan Mayer, Steve Gottlieb, Bob Davis, Sam and Nancy Armato, Judy Stakee, Linda Newmark, Mike Rosen, LaRonda Sutton, Lizzy Moore, Natalie and Jonathan Firstenberg, Lou and Almiede Arnell, Kenny and Tracy Bailey, Marietta Kin, Robin Dimaggio, P. G. Sturges, Rebecca Chavira, Zach Katz, Bob Davis, Elio and Anthony Armato, Sandy Sturges, and Karen Otto: Thank you all for reading and discussing early drafts and for guiding me with your suggestions and reactions.

Lastly, thank you to all my friends and colleagues who have supported and encouraged me throughout, especially David Renzer, Jeff Jampol, Lenny Beer, Gary Stiffelman, Bruce Goldstein, Peter Thall, Avery Lipman, Michael McDonald, Pat Higdon, Diana Baron, and Phin Daly.

A portion of the proceeds of this book will be donated to the Witness to a Dream Foundation (Regina Boutte, president), a charitable organization dedicated to encouraging, recognizing, and rewarding mentoring (www.witnesstoadream.org).

TOM STURGES
Manhattan Beach, California

ABOUT THE AUTHOR

TOM STURGES is the father of two sons, now ages ten and sixteen. He is executive vice president and head of creative affairs for Universal Music Publishing. He is a coach, mentor, teacher, and volunteer. His efforts with at-risk children at an inner city Los Angeles public school have impacted the lives of hundreds of students there. He has received fourteen commendations from civic and national leaders for his volunteerism, which is also the topic of the forthcoming documentary *Witness to a Dream*. Sturges's father was the legendary filmmaker Preston Sturges. Tom Sturges lives in Manhattan Beach, California.